CONVERSATIONS BETWEEN WOMEN

A Comprehensive Guide To Decipher the Female Code, Think Like a Woman, and Build a Lasting Relationship with Her

.

NICCI BROCHARD
&
DR. BEN CHUBA

CONVERSATIONS BETWEEN WOMEN

A Comprehensive Guide To Decipher the Female Code, Think Like a Woman, and Build a Lasting Relationship with Her

CROSSBORDER

New York, London, Quebec

Also published by Nicci Brochard and Dr. Ben Chuba

1. *Managing Your Subconscious Mind And Emotions: Techniques To Resist Negativity, Stay Focused, Be Positive, And Find Happiness In Daily Activities.*

2. *From paycheck to payday: How To Make Money Last Longer In Your Pocket, Understand The Mind, Measure Money, And Build Everlasting Wealth.*

3. *When Decluttering Is Not An Option: Techniques To Reimagine & Reinvent Your Space And Yourself With Less Stress, Anxiety, And Freedom From Perfectionism.*

4. *Mind-blowing Fun facts about marriage and Divorce : "I Now Pronounce You Fun & F*cked", Marriage & Divorce Facts Not Taught at the Altar-With Interpretations and Moral Lessons*

5. *Conversations Between Men: A Comprehensive Guide To Decipher The Male Code, Think Like A Man, And Build A Lasting Relationship With Him.*

6. *Social Savviness For Teens And Young Adults: A Modern Guide To Overcoming Social Media Traps, Anxiety, Peer Pressure, And The Fear Of Missing Out.*

CONTENTS

Forward

For centuries, men have pondered the mysteries of the female mind, often feeling lost in translation when understanding what women genuinely mean, want, and need. Conversations with women can feel like navigating an intricate maze; one wrong turn, and suddenly, what seemed like a casual chat has transformed into an emotional minefield.

But what if you could finally decode the language of women? What if you could decipher the words and the deeper emotions and intentions behind them? What if you could connect with women in a way that fosters trust, understanding, and attraction?

This book is your guide to doing exactly that. It is not just about understanding what women say, it's about thinking like a woman, embracing emotional intelligence, and fostering genuine, lasting connections. Whether you're dating, in a long-term relationship, or simply trying to improve your communication with the women in your life, the principles outlined here will help you master the art of female conversations.

In these pages, you'll discover:

- The subtle cues and unspoken signals women use to communicate.

- How we can differentiate between what she says and what she means?

- The key to making her feel genuinely heard and understood.

- The emotional triggers that build trust, intimacy, and connection.

This is not about manipulation or playing games; it's about cultivating a deeper, more authentic understanding of women. Once you learn to interpret the female code, you'll communicate better and build stronger, more meaningful relationships that stand the test of time.

Are you ready to think like a woman and revolutionize how you connect with her? Well, come along and we (Nicci and Ben) will show you how.

CHAPTER 1

Understanding The Female Communication Style

The Brain, the Voice, and the Connection

D id you know that, on average, women use around **20,000 words per day**, while men use only about **7,000**? This widely cited statistic, though debated, highlights a fascinating reality; women generally communicate more frequently and with more nuance than men. But why is that the case? Is it a biological difference, a cultural norm, or something deeper rooted in human evolution?

To truly grasp how and why women communicate the way they do, we must explore the science behind female communication, the role of emotional intelligence, and the impact of tone, nuance, and body language. Additionally, societal, and cultural factors shape how women express themselves.

By the end of this chapter, you'll better understand the complex, multi-layered nature of female communication and why mastering it can lead to stronger relationships, better workplace dynamics, and deeper personal connections.

The Science Behind Female Communication

The Brain and Language Processing

One of the most significant differences between male and female communication styles is brain function. Neuroscience research has shown that women use both hemispheres of their brains when processing language, whereas men primarily engage the left hemisphere.

This ability to utilize both hemispheres enables women to:

- Process **words and emotions simultaneously**, allowing for greater emotional depth in conversation.

- Interpret **verbal and non-verbal cues** more effectively.

- Engage in **more detailed and context-driven communication** rather than purely factual exchanges.

The Role of Hormones

Another contributing factor is **hormonal influence**. Estrogen, a dominant female hormone, enhances verbal ability and emotional sensitivity, making women naturally more attuned to subtleties in speech. More prevalent in men, testosterone promotes directness and assertiveness, often leading to **a more straightforward communication style**.

Evolutionary Perspectives

From an evolutionary standpoint, communication in women has always been essential for **building social bonds and maintaining group cohesion**. Early human societies relied on women for gathering, childbearing, and maintaining relationships within the tribe, which required **strong interpersonal skills**. Men, by contrast, were more engaged in hunting and territorial defense, favoring a more **concise, action-oriented form of communication**.

These biological and evolutionary differences are still apparent in modern interactions, influencing how men and women express thoughts, feelings, and needs.

Emotional Intelligence and Its Role in Female Conversations

What is Emotional Intelligence?

Emotional intelligence (EI) is the ability to recognize, understand, manage, and influence emotions in oneself and others. Women, on average, score **higher** in emotional intelligence than men, particularly in the domains of:

- **Empathy** (understanding others' emotions)

- **Social awareness** (reading social cues)

- **Relationship management** (navigating interpersonal dynamics)

This high level of emotional intelligence affects how women communicate in several ways.

The Power of Empathy in Communication

Empathy is central to **female discourse**, allowing for **deep listening and validation**. Women tend to prioritize emotional connection over simply **exchanging information**, which is why:

- They often **mirror emotions**, using phrases like "I understand" or "That must be hard."

- Conversations may include more **questions** to show interest, such as "How did that make you feel?"

- They use **affirmative sounds** (e.g., "Mmm-hmm," "Oh wow") to signal engagement.

This emotional attunement makes conversations with women more layered, as they focus on **how something is being said as much as what is being said.**

Conflict Resolution Through Emotional Intelligence

Unlike men, who often approach conflict **logically and solution-oriented**, women handle disputes through **relational and emotional understanding**. Instead of immediately offering a solution, they may:

- Express **concern for how the other person feels** before addressing the problem.

- Use **inclusive language** ("We should figure this out together") rather than **directive speech** ("You need to fix this").

- Prefer **harmony over confrontation**, aiming to de-escalate rather than escalate tension.

Understanding this emotional intelligence-driven communication style is crucial for **resolving conflicts effectively and fostering positive relationships**.

The Importance of Nuance, Tone, and Body Language

Nuance: The Art of Subtlety

Women often communicate using **subtext**, which means they may not always say precisely what they mean outright. Instead, meaning is **woven into tone, choice of words, and body language**.

For instance, a simple **"I'm fine"** can have multiple meanings depending on:

- The tone (soft, sharp, sarcastic, distant)

- The facial expression (smile, frown, blank stare)

- The context (spoken after an argument vs. in a neutral setting)

This nuanced way of speaking allows women to **convey multiple layers of meaning simultaneously**, making conversations rich and emotionally charged.

The Power of Tone

Tone carries just as much weight as words. Women may use a **gentle tone to convey warmth**, a **sharp tone to assert boundaries**, or a **playful tone to add humor**. Because of this, **misinterpretations** often arise when someone fails to read between the lines.

A common example:

- A woman says, **"Oh, don't worry about it,"** in a **flat tone—** which could signal annoyance, dismissal, or genuine reassurance.

- If said in a **cheerful tone**, it likely means she honestly isn't bothered.

This complexity in tone is **why emails, text messages, and online communication** can sometimes lead to misunderstandings; **without vocal cues, the intended meaning can be lost**.

Body Language: The Unspoken Words

Women rely heavily on **non-verbal communication**, often **synchronizing their body language with their emotions**. They tend to:

- **Maintain eye contact** to show interest and connection.

- **Use more facial expressions** to convey feelings.

- **To indicate attentiveness, engage in physical gestures, like nodding or leaning in.**

Because body language is crucial, reading these cues correctly can **significantly improve interpersonal communication**.

How Societal and Cultural Factors Shape Women's Communication Styles

Social Conditioning and Gender Expectations

From a young age, women are often encouraged to:

- **Be polite and accommodating** ("Don't be too aggressive.")

- **Prioritize relationships** over self-interest.

- **Express emotions freely** (but in a controlled manner).

Conversely, men are often socialized to be **direct, assertive, and competitive** in speech. These early influences create different **communication expectations**, making female conversation styles more **collaborative** than **confrontational**.

Workplace Communication: Challenges and Adaptations

In professional settings, women often **adjust their communication style** to balance warmth and authority. Studies show that:

- Women **use more hedging language** ("I think," "Maybe we should") to avoid appearing too forceful.

- They **soften criticism** by offering **positive reinforcement first**.

- They **rely on consensus-building** rather than dictating decisions.

While these approaches foster collaboration, they can sometimes lead to **women being perceived as less authoritative**, which is why many professionals work to **strike a balance between warmth and assertiveness**.

Cultural Influences on Female Communication

Culture plays a significant role in shaping how women communicate. For example:

- In **Western cultures**, women are encouraged to be more vocal and expressive.

- In **Eastern cultures**, there is often a greater emphasis on **indirect communication and deference**.

- In **Latin cultures**, women's speech tends to be more **animated and expressive**, reflecting passionate communication norms.

Understanding these cultural differences helps avoid **misinterpretations in cross-cultural interactions**.

Final Thoughts: The Beauty of Female Communication

Women's communication style blends **science, emotion, nuance, and cultural influence**. It is dynamic, wealthy, and deeply connected to human relationships. Understanding the biological, psychological, and social factors that shape it can improve communication across genders and strengthen personal and professional relationships.

The next time you find yourself in a conversation with a woman, pay attention to **the tone, the nuance, the body language**, and the emotional undercurrent. You may discover far more being said than just the words alone.

CHAPTER 2

The Power of Connection: Why Women Talk

The Science of Connection: Why Women Are Wired to Communicate

From an evolutionary perspective, communication was a survival strategy. In early human societies, while men focused on hunting and providing, women cultivated strong social networks to nurture their communities and children. Language was their lifeline; a way to share wisdom, warn of dangers, and foster cooperation. Today, this deep-rooted inclination remains, shaping the way women connect.

So, why do women talk? Not just for the sake of it. Conversation, for women, is rarely just about exchanging information; it's about **forming relationships, processing emotions, and reinforcing trust**. Understanding the dynamics of how and why women communicate can transform relationships, friendships, and even workplaces.

Communication as a Tool for Emotional Bonding

For many women, talking isn't just about words—it's about connection. A conversation can be as meaningful as a hug, a sign of solidarity, or an act of emotional intimacy. While men often use communication to exchange facts and solve problems, women lean on it to **express feelings, release stress, and deepen relationships**.

From childhood, girls are socialized to value relationships through conversation. They engage in more **face-to-face interactions**, sharing stories, discussing feelings, and offering support. These interactions create oxytocin, often called the **"love hormone,"** which fosters trust and deepens bonds. This chemical reaction is why heart-to-heart talks can feel so fulfilling.

Moreover, the rhythm of female conversation often mirrors a dance. It involves **mirroring emotions, exchanging nonverbal cues, and responding with empathy**. When one woman shares a problematic experience, the listener frequently responds with phrases like, *"I know exactly how you feel"* or *"That must have been so frustrating."* This kind of response **validates emotions** and strengthens the connection between them.

The Difference Between Venting and Seeking Solutions

One of the biggest misunderstandings between men and women in communication lies in the difference between **venting** and **problem-solving**.

When a woman expresses frustration about a tough day at work, a disagreement with a friend, or a stressful situation, she often isn't looking for an immediate solution; she's looking for an **outlet to process her emotions**. Talking helps organize thoughts and make sense of experiences.

However, in mixed-gender conversations, men often assume that when a woman talks about a problem, she is seeking advice. This can lead to responses like:

- "Why don't you just talk to your boss about it?"

- "You should stop worrying so much."

- "I think you're overreacting."

While well-intentioned, these statements can leave a woman feeling unheard or dismissed. What she seeks in these moments is **understanding, not a quick fix**.

Women have an innate ability to **co-regulate emotions** through conversation. A sense of emotional relief activates when a friend listens and acknowledges her feelings. This is why, after a long chat, women often say, *"I feel so much better just talking to you."* Verbalizing emotions allows them to be processed rather than bottled up.

On the flip side, when a woman is looking for a solution, she might **ask for it directly**. Recognizing the difference between these two modes of communication can significantly enhance relationships.

How to Tell the Difference:

- If she says, *"I just need to vent,"* she likely needs a listening ear.

- If she asks, *"What do you think I should do?"* she seeks advice.

- If she expresses frustration but doesn't ask for input, she's likely in **emotional processing mode**, and the best response is validation.

Why Validation Matters More Than Fixing the Problem

Validation is a fundamental human need, yet it's often underestimated. In communication, especially among women, **feeling heard is more important than hearing a solution**.

Validation means acknowledging someone's emotions and making them feel understood. It doesn't mean agreeing with everything they say, it simply means recognizing their feelings as valid.

The Power of "I Hear You"

Imagine a woman comes home and says:

"I had the worst day at work. My boss ignored my ideas, and my coworker took credit for my project."

A **fix-it response** would be

"You should confront your coworker and make sure your boss knows the truth."

A **validating response** would be:

"That sounds incredibly frustrating. You put so much work into that project, and it's unfair that someone else is taking the credit."

Which one feels better? Most women would choose the second response. Validation acknowledges the **emotional experience** and makes her feel heard.

This concept applies to romantic relationships and extends to friendships, family dynamics, and professional settings. Leaders who validate the concerns of female employees create stronger team morale. Friends who validate each other build deeper bonds. **The power of validation cannot be overstated.**

Building Trust Through Active Listening and Shared Experiences

Trust is the foundation of any meaningful relationship, and one of the best ways to build it is through **active listening**.

Active listening is more than just hearing words; it's about **engaging fully** in the conversation. This means:

- Making eye contact

- Nodding or using affirming responses (*"That makes sense,"* *"Tell me more"*)

- Refraining from interrupting

- Asking thoughtful follow-up questions

Women value depth in conversation. Unlike surface-level exchanges, **deep and meaningful discussions** create an emotional connection that fosters long-term trust.

The Role of Shared Experiences

Another cornerstone of female communication is **shared experiences**. Women often bond over everyday struggles, whether navigating career challenges, motherhood, or personal growth. This explains why women's support groups and friendships frequently become so strong; a mutual "I understand you" energy builds trust.

For instance, a mother struggling with postpartum challenges may find immense comfort in talking to another mother who has experienced the same thing. A woman going through a career shift might find reassurance in a friend who has faced a similar transition. **Shared experiences reinforce empathy, making communication even more powerful.**

Final Thoughts: Embracing the Power of Female Communication

Women don't just talk for the sake of talking. They speak to **heal, connect, understand, and be understood**. Conversation is their way of expressing love, offering support, and processing the world around them.

Understanding the purpose behind female communication allows for **stronger relationships, better workplaces, and deeper friendships**. Whether through venting, validation or simply sharing life's experiences, the power of conversation remains one of the most essential and beautiful aspects of female connection.

So, the next time a woman opens up about her thoughts, she should resist the urge to fix the problem immediately. Instead, listen, validate, and connect; that's where the real magic happens.

CHAPTER 3

The Hidden Meanings in Conversations

"The most important thing in communication is hearing what isn't said." – Peter Drucker

The Art of Reading Between the Lines

Communication is far more than words alone. It is an intricate dance of verbal phrasing, tone, body language, and context that conveys meaning beyond what is explicitly spoken. While direct communication can be simple and unambiguous, many conversations, especially those involving emotions, carry an unspoken subtext that requires careful interpretation.

Understanding what someone truly means requires an awareness of their choice of words, how they say them, and their accompanying physical cues. This is particularly significant in conversations with women, where indirect communication is key. Knowing how to distinguish between what is said and what is meant can make all the difference in social interactions, dating, and relationships.

What She Says vs. What She Means

Women, like anyone else, use words as one component of communication. However, societal expectations and emotional intelligence often lead them to rely more on subtleties and implications than blunt statements. This can sometimes create a gap between what is expressed verbally and what is meant.

For example, consider these common phrases and their potential meanings:

- **"I'm fine."** – This does not always mean she is okay. It could signal that she is upset but does not want to discuss it now. Paying attention to her tone, facial expressions, and whether she avoids eye contact can provide clarity.

- **"Do whatever you want."** – While it may sound like permission, it often carries an undertone of disappointment or frustration, suggesting that she prefers an inevitable outcome but does not want to demand it explicitly.

- **"Nothing's wrong."** – This can sometimes be a protective shield, signaling that something is wrong, but she may be waiting for you to show concern or inquire further.

- **"I don't want to talk about it right now."** – This could mean she genuinely needs time to process her emotions, or it could be a test to see if you care enough to dig deeper.

These nuances highlight the importance of context and emotional intelligence in interpreting conversations. The key is not to assume but to observe, ask thoughtful questions, and engage with sincerity.

Verbal and Non-Verbal Cues of Affection, Frustration, or Disinterest

Words alone rarely tell the whole story. Body language, facial expressions, tone of voice, and even pauses in speech play a critical role in conveying emotions and intentions.

Signs of Affection

- **Leaning In:** A sign of engagement and interest, especially when combined with sustained eye contact.

- **Mirroring Movements:** Subtly imitating your gestures or posture is a subconscious way of creating a connection.

- **Light Touches:** A gentle touch on the arm or shoulder indicates warmth and comfort.

- **Frequent Smiling and Eye Contact:** Holding eye contact longer than usual can signal attraction and interest.

Signs of Frustration

- **Crossed Arms:** A defensive or closed-off stance that could indicate disagreement or discomfort.

- **Short Responses:** Curt's answers often suggest irritation, disinterest, or emotional withdrawal.

- **Avoiding Eye Contact:** If she looks away frequently or doesn't maintain focus, it could signal frustration or evasion.

- **Exaggerated Sighs or Eye Rolls:** Classic indicators of annoyance or impatience.

Signs of Disinterest

- **Lack of Engagement:** One-word answers, delayed responses, or a distracted demeanor can mean disengagement.

- **Checking the Time or Phone:** A clear sign that her attention is elsewhere, and she may not be interested in the conversation.

- **Turning Her Body Away:** Physical orientation is a significant cue; turning away suggests discomfort or the desire to exit the interaction.

- **Politeness Without Enthusiasm:** If she engages in conversation but does so out of courtesy rather than genuine interest, it's usually evident in her tone and lack of enthusiasm.

By being mindful of these cues, one can better navigate conversations, ensuring that responses align with the emotional context of the moment.

The Power of Indirect Communication and Subtle Hints

Subtext plays a crucial role in communication. Indirect speech allows people to express thoughts or feelings non-confrontationally, preserving harmony while conveying deeper meaning.

Women, in particular, may use subtle hints rather than outright statements, especially in sensitive discussions. These hints can manifest as:

- **Implying Rather Than Stating:** Instead of saying, "I want to spend more time with you," she may say, "You're always so busy lately."

- **Framing Feelings as Questions:** "Do you think we should go out this weekend?" may mean, "I want to spend quality time together."

- **Using Humor or Sarcasm:** Playful remarks or sarcastic comments can sometimes mask true feelings, requiring more profound attention to context and delivery.

These indirect methods are often used to test reactions, gauge interest, or avoid outright rejection. Recognizing and addressing these hints can help strengthen communication and avoid misunderstandings.

The Role of Context in Deciphering Meaning

Context shapes communication in fundamental ways. The exact phrase can have vastly different meanings depending on the setting, mood, and speaker relationship.

Consider the following scenarios:

- **In a Casual Setting:** If she says, "I don't need anything," when you offer her a drink at a party, she may genuinely mean it.

- **In an Emotional Moment,** If the exact phrase is spoken during a conflict, it might convey, "I want you to insist or show that you care."

- **Over Text vs. In-Person:** Text messages lack vocal tone and body language, making them easily misinterpreted. A simple 'Okay." via text might seem neutral, but in person, with a clipped tone, it could indicate annoyance.

Understanding the broader situation allows for a more accurate interpretation of meaning.

Final Thoughts: Becoming a Master of Conversation

Recognizing hidden meanings in conversations requires practice, patience, and genuine attentiveness. It involves:

- **Listening Actively:** Focus not just on words but on tone, expression, and physical cues.

- **Asking Clarifying Questions:** When in doubt, gently probe for more information rather than assuming.

- **Observing Patterns:** Everyone has unique communication styles. Recognizing patterns in someone's speech and behavior over time can make it easier to understand their unspoken messages.

- **Being Emotionally Intelligent:** Empathy and awareness of emotional context enhance one's ability to interpret meaning accurately.

Mastering these skills can lead to deeper connections, fewer misunderstandings, and more meaningful interactions. As the famous adage goes, "It's not just what you say, but how you say it."

CHAPTER 4

Emotional Triggers and How to Navigate Them

"The greatest weapon against stress is our ability to choose one thought over another." – William James

Understanding Emotional Triggers

Emotional triggers are deeply ingrained responses to words, actions, or situations that evoke strong emotional reactions. These triggers often stem from past experiences, societal pressures, or deeply held personal values. For women, emotional triggers can be particularly complex due to a multitude of social, cultural, and psychological influences.

Topics that carry deep emotional weight for women are often rooted in experiences of self-worth, safety, relationships, societal expectations, and personal identity. Whether it's a comment about body image, discussions surrounding work-life balance, or remarks about emotional expression, these triggers can elicit strong responses that affect interactions and relationships. Understanding these triggers and why they evoke such reactions is the first step in navigating them effectively.

Common Emotional Triggers for Women

While emotional triggers vary from person to person, several common topics tend to hold deep emotional weight for many women:

1. **Body Image and Self-Worth** – Conversations surrounding physical appearance can be particularly sensitive. Remarks about weight, ageing, or beauty standards can inadvertently tap into deep-seated insecurities or past experiences of judgment.

2. **Career and Ambition** – Many women face societal pressure regarding their career choices. Comments about work-life balance, leadership capabilities, or success in male-dominated fields can trigger emotions tied to personal achievement and societal expectations.

3. **Relationships and Family Expectations** – Questions or judgments about marriage, motherhood, and relationships can stir feelings of frustration, inadequacy, or pressure.

4. **Emotional Sensitivity** – The stereotype that women are 'too emotional' can be profoundly frustrating and triggering, often leading to feelings of being dismissed or invalidated.

5. **Past Trauma and Personal Experiences** – Past experiences of discrimination, abuse, or hardship can resurface unintentionally in conversations, leading to strong emotional reactions.

Recognizing Emotional Shifts

One of the most critical aspects of navigating emotional triggers is recognizing when emotions begin to shift. These shifts may not always be overtly expressed, but subtle cues in body language, tone, or expression can indicate a change in emotional state.

Signs to look out for include:

- **Sudden silence or withdrawal** – If someone previously engaged in conversation suddenly becomes quiet, it may be a sign that they feel uncomfortable or triggered.

- **Changes in tone or body language** – A shift in tone from relaxed to defensive, crossed arms, or avoiding eye contact can signal emotional distress.

- **Over-explaining or justifying** – When someone feels emotionally triggered, they may need to justify their feelings or reactions more than usual.

- **Sharp responses or sarcasm** – A sudden use of sarcasm or defensive remarks can indicate underlying emotional discomfort.

Recognizing these signals allows for more compassionate and thoughtful interactions, helping prevent misunderstandings before they escalate.

Responding to Emotional Shifts

Once an emotional shift is recognized, responding with sensitivity and understanding is key. A few strategies can help navigate these situations smoothly:

1. **Acknowledge Feelings Without Judgment** – Instead of dismissing emotions, validate them. A simple "I can see that

this is an important topic for you" can go a long way in making someone feel heard.

2. **Ask Open-Ended Questions** – Instead of making assumptions, ask questions like, "Can you tell me more about how you feel?" This encourages communication without forcing an immediate response.

3. **Practice Active Listening** – Give undivided attention, maintain eye contact, and refrain from interrupting. Reflecting on what has been said can also show that you genuinely listen.

4. **Maintain a Calm and Supportive Demeanor** – Keeping your tone calm and composed helps prevent the situation from escalating further.

5. **Allow Space if Needed** – If emotions are running high, sometimes the best response is to give someone space to process their feelings before continuing the conversation.

The Art of De-Escalating Tension Without Dismissing Feelings

When emotions are heightened, de-escalation is crucial to maintaining a constructive dialogue. However, de-escalation does not mean dismissing or invalidating emotions—it is about creating an environment where the conversation can proceed productively.

Techniques for De-Escalation

1. **Remain Neutral and Compassionate** – Avoid responding with heightened emotions yourself. Keeping a calm and steady demeanor helps set the tone for the conversation.

2. **Use "I" Statements Instead of "You" Statements** – Statements like "I feel that this topic is important to you" are less likely to be perceived as confrontational compared to "You're getting too emotional about this."

3. **Find Common Ground** – Identifying shared values or experiences can help diffuse tension. "I completely understand why this matters to you" can help create a connection.

4. **Take Breaks When Necessary** – Suggesting a break can allow both parties to regroup and return with a clearer perspective if a conversation is too emotionally charged.

5. **Avoid Defensiveness** – Avoid getting defensive Even if you disagree with the reaction. Instead, focus on understanding the root of the emotion.

Avoiding Common Conversational Pitfalls

Certain conversational habits can unintentionally escalate emotional situations rather than diffuse them. Avoiding these pitfalls can lead to healthier discussions:

1. **Minimizing Feelings** – Saying things like "You're overreacting" or "It's not a big deal" can make someone feel unheard and invalidated.

2. **Interrupting or Talking Over Someone** – Cutting someone off while expressing their emotions can heighten frustration and lead to further disengagement.

3. **Offering Unsolicited Advice Too Quickly** – Sometimes, people want to be heard rather than immediately provided a solution. Asking, "Would you like advice or just a listening ear?" can be helpful.

4. **Comparing Experiences** – Statements like "I went through the same thing, and I got over it" can feel dismissive. Instead, focus on acknowledging their unique experience.

5. **Blaming or Shaming** – Assigning blame, whether directly or indirectly, can push emotions higher. Instead of "You always get upset about this," try "I see that this is important to you."

Cultivating Emotional Awareness and Empathy

Navigating emotional triggers effectively requires cultivating emotional intelligence, awareness, and empathy. Understanding that each person's experiences shape their emotional responses helps create a more compassionate approach to communication.

Practicing mindfulness, self-reflection, and educating oneself about emotional intelligence can enhance the ability to navigate emotionally charged situations. By recognizing triggers, responding with empathy, and fostering open and honest conversations, emotional triggers can become an opportunity for deeper understanding rather than a source of conflict.

Mastering the art of navigating emotional triggers fosters more substantial, compassionate relationships. In personal or professional settings, approaching emotionally charged conversations with sensitivity and respect leads to deeper connections and mutual understanding.

CHAPTER 5

Conflict and Resolution: How Women Handle Disagreements

"Peace is not the absence of conflict, but the ability to cope with it." — Mahatma Gandhi

Understanding the Female Approach to Conflict

onflict is an inevitable aspect of human relationships, and how individuals handle disagreements can shape the nature of their interactions. Women, on average, tend to approach conflicts differently than men due to a combination of social conditioning, emotional intelligence, and interpersonal priorities. While men often view conflict as a competitive challenge—one to be won or lost—women frequently see it as an opportunity to deepen connections, foster understanding, and preserve harmony.

From childhood, many girls are socialized to prioritize relationships and emotional attunement, leading to a preference for resolution strategies that emphasize empathy and compromise. This inclination often contrasts with the more direct and confrontational approach encouraged in boys, who are typically taught to assert dominance and defend their viewpoints unequivocally. Rather than seeking a clear-cut victory in an argument, women often navigate disputes to maintain or strengthen the relationship.

The biological aspect also plays a role in shaping how women handle disagreements. Studies indicate that women have a heightened response in the brain regions associated with emotional processing, allowing for greater sensitivity to relational nuances during conflicts. This can contribute to an approach that is less about asserting power and more about managing emotions and fostering mutual understanding.

Confrontational vs. Collaborative Problem-Solving

One of the fundamental distinctions in conflict resolution is the contrast between confrontational and collaborative problem-solving.

Confrontational Problem-Solving. This style is characterized by a direct, sometimes aggressive approach, where the primary goal is to establish dominance or secure a specific outcome. In a confrontational model, conflict is seen as a battleground in which each party fights for their interests, often without concern for the relational cost. This approach may be more common in male-dominated settings where hierarchical structures reinforce assertiveness as a means of resolution.

In contrast, collaborative problem-solving prioritizes communication, active listening, and mutual compromise. Women are more likely to employ this method, aiming for a solution that benefits all parties involved rather than a win-lose dynamic. This approach requires patience, empathy, and a willingness to consider multiple perspectives, making it especially effective in sustaining long-term relationships.

Collaboration also involves understanding emotional intelligence; the ability to recognize, interpret, and regulate emotions in oneself and others. Women tend to excel in this domain, using emotional cues to gauge the direction of a conversation and adapt their responses accordingly. This ability to read between the lines, pick up on underlying tensions, and offer reassurances can prevent a disagreement from escalating into a damaging confrontation.

Diffusing Arguments While Keeping the Conversation Productive

Even the most adept communicators can find themselves in heated disagreements. Maintaining composure and steering the conversation toward a constructive resolution is the key to handling such situations. Below are strategies women often use to diffuse tension and keep discussions productive:

1. **Active Listening and Validation.** Before responding to a disagreement, women often prioritize understanding the other person's perspective. Using active listening techniques, such as nodding, paraphrasing, and making affirming statements ("I see what you're saying" or "That must have been frustrating for you"), can help de-escalate emotions and create an environment where both parties feel heard.

2. **Avoiding Escalation Through Emotional Regulation.** Emotional responses can either fuel or diffuse a conflict. Women often use calming strategies such as taking deep breaths, speaking in measured tones, and using non-threatening body language to control an escalating situation.

3. **Choosing Words Carefully.** Language plays a critical role in conflict resolution. Women tend to favor "I" statements over "you" r" statements to avoid placing blame and triggering defensiveness. For example, saying "I felt hurt when this happened" rather than "You made me feel hurt" fosters openness rather than resistance.

4. **Using Humor and Lightheartedness.** Strategic humor can be a powerful tool in de-escalating tension. A well-

placed joke or playful remark can defuse defensiveness and help both parties gain perspective. However, humor should be used carefully, ensuring it does not dismiss the other person's concerns.

5. **Offering Solutions Rather Than Focusing on the Problem.** Instead of dwelling on the disagreement, women often focus on finding a solution that benefits both parties. This proactive approach transforms conflict from a source of division into an opportunity for growth.

6. **Taking a Break if Necessary.** Sometimes, emotions run too high for productive conversation. Women may suggest temporarily stepping away from the discussion to allow both parties to cool down and collect their thoughts. This prevents impulsive reactions that could damage the relationship.

Rebuilding Trust and Strengthening Bonds After a Disagreement

Resolving a conflict is only half the battle; the actual test of a relationship lies in how trust is rebuilt afterwards. Women emphasize emotional repair following disagreements, ensuring unresolved resentment does not linger. Here are some of the ways they achieve this:

1. **Acknowledging the Other Person's Feelings.** Expressing genuine understanding, and accepting any hurt caused during the disagreement can go a long way in mending relationships. A simple "I understand why that upset you, and I'm sorry" can be incredibly healing.

2. **Reaffirming Commitment to the Relationship.** Whether in a romantic relationship, friendship, or workplace

dynamic, verbal reassurance of commitment helps restore security. Women often use phrases like "I value our relationship, and I don't want this to come between us" to emphasize the importance of maintaining the bond.

3. **Small Gestures of Reconciliation.** Actions often speak louder than words. Offering a cup of coffee, sending a thoughtful text, or planning an activity together can be a non-verbal way of showing a willingness to move forward positively.

4. **Learning from the Conflict** Women often reflect on disagreements to understand what triggered them and how similar situations can be handled better in the future. This introspective approach helps prevent recurring conflicts and fosters emotional growth.

5. **Letting Go of Resentment.** Holding onto past grievances can be toxic to any relationship. Women often employ journaling, meditation, or open conversations to process emotions and let go of lingering negativity.

Conclusion

Women's approach to conflict resolution is often shaped by a blend of emotional intelligence, social conditioning, and a deep-seated desire to preserve relationships. By focusing on collaborative problem-solving, active listening, and emotional regulation, women can transform disagreements into opportunities for connection and growth. Ultimately, navigating conflict with empathy and understanding strengthens bonds, proving that disagreements—when handled effectively—can lead to even greater trust and intimacy.

CHAPTER 6

Conversations in Romantic Relationships

"The single biggest problem in communication is the illusion that it has taken place." – George Bernard Shaw.

Communication is the heartbeat of romantic relationships. How partners express their thoughts, feelings, and concerns determines the emotional climate of the relationship. While both men and women bring unique communication styles to the table, this chapter delves into how women, in particular, express love and affection, the necessity of reassurance, the importance of effectively communicating needs and boundaries, and the role of clarity in avoiding misunderstandings that could lead to emotional distance.

How Women Express Love and Affection Through Words

Women often use verbal communication as a primary way to express love and affection. While actions are undeniably necessary, words are a powerful bridge to emotional connection. Unlike stereotypical portrayals that suggest women are excessively emotional or verbose, research indicates that women generally have a more relational approach to communication.

The Power of Affirmations

Women frequently use affirmations to express love. Simple phrases like:

- I appreciate everything you do for me.

- I feel so lucky to have you in my life.

- You make my day better just by being in it.

These affirmations create a sense of warmth and connection. They serve as verbal reminders of affection, reassurance, and appreciation. According to psychologist Gary Chapman, author of *The Five Love Languages*, words of affirmation are one of the most common ways people give and receive love, and women tend to use them frequently to nurture emotional intimacy.

Storytelling and Emotional Sharing

Another way women express affection is through storytelling. They share personal stories, childhood memories, or funny moments from their day. This conversation is casual chatter and an invitation into their inner world. By sharing experiences, they seek to strengthen the emotional bond with their partner.

Subtle Cues in Conversations

Women may also express love through small verbal cues such as checking in:

- Did you eat today?

- Are you okay? You seemed a little off earlier.

- Let me know when you get home safely.

These simple phrases may seem routine but communicate deep care and concern. They reflect a desire to ensure their partner's well-being and create a nurturing atmosphere in the relationship.

The Importance of Reassurance and Emotional Security

Reassurance is a fundamental aspect of communication in romantic relationships. For many women, verbal affirmations of love and commitment serve as anchors that provide emotional security.

Why Reassurance Matters

Insecure or inconsistent communication can create doubts, even in stable relationships. Reassurance helps dissolve unnecessary anxieties and reinforces trust. This doesn't mean that women constantly need validation; periodic affirmations help sustain the emotional connection.

Ways partners can provide reassurance:

1. **Verbal Affection** – Saying "I love you" or "I'm here for you" sincerely and often.

2. **Consistency** – Following through on promises and maintaining open communication.

3. **Nonverbal Gestures** – A reassuring touch, a warm hug, or a gentle hand squeeze.

4. **Attentive Listening** – Making an effort to hear and understand without dismissing feelings.

Reassurance vs. Over-Dependency

While reassurance is healthy, excessive dependence on validation can create an imbalance. It is essential that both partners feel secure within themselves and the relationship. Open communication about fears, expectations, and emotional needs can help prevent one-sided reassurance patterns.

Communicating Needs, Desires, and Boundaries Effectively

Clear communication of needs and boundaries is crucial in romantic relationships. When partners openly discuss what they need, misunderstandings are minimized, and mutual respect is strengthened.

Understanding and Expressing Needs

Every person has unique emotional and physical needs in a relationship. Some require more time, while others prioritize physical affection or deep conversations. Women often communicate their needs indirectly, hoping their partner will intuitively pick up on them. However, unspoken expectations can lead to disappointment.

How to Communicate Needs Clearly:

1. **Use "I" Statements** – Instead of saying, *"You never spend time with me,"* rephrase it as *"I feel loved when we spend quality time together."*

2. **Be Direct Yet Compassionate** – Honesty does not have to be harsh. Clearly stating what you need kindly helps avoid conflict

3. **Express Needs as Requests, Not Demands** – Saying, *"I would love if we could have more date nights,"* is more effective than, *"You should take me out more."*

Setting Healthy Boundaries

Boundaries are essential for maintaining respect and balance. They define what is acceptable and what is not, helping both partners feel safe and understood.

Examples of Relationship Boundaries:

- **Emotional Boundaries:** *"I need time alone when I'm overwhelmed; it helps me process my feelings."*

- **Communication Boundaries:** *"I don't feel comfortable discussing personal arguments in front of others."*

- **Physical Boundaries:** *"I prefer not to be hugged when upset; I need a moment first."*

Respecting and communicating boundaries creates a safe space for intimacy to grow.

Avoiding Misinterpretations That Lead to Emotional Distance

Miscommunication can be one of the biggest threats to emotional closeness in relationships. Even well-intended words can be misinterpreted, leading to unnecessary tension.

Common Communication Pitfalls

1. **Assuming Instead of Asking**

   o Instead of assuming a partner's behavior means something negative, asking clarifying questions can prevent misunderstandings.

   o Example: Instead of *"You don't care about me,"* try *"I noticed you've been quiet today. Is something on your mind?"*

2. **Reading Too Much into Tone or Texts**

   o   In digital communication, lack of tone and body language can create confusion. A simple *"Okay."* text may be read as cold, even if the sender didn't intend it that way.

   o   Solution: Avoid overanalyzing messages and opt for face-to-face or phone conversations when discussing serious matters.

3. **Bringing Up Past Conflicts Unnecessarily**

   o   Rehashing past issues during disagreements can make conversations feel like battles rather than constructive discussions.

   o   Solution: Focus on resolving the present issue rather than stacking grievances.

How to Foster Clear and Loving Communication

- **Practice Active Listening** – Giving undivided attention when a partner speaks fosters a deeper connection.

- **Use Positive Language** – Framing conversations constructively strengthens relationships.

- **Clarify Intentions** – If something seems off, seeking clarification helps prevent unnecessary conflicts.

Final Thoughts: The Art of Loving Conversations

Conversations in romantic relationships are about words, connection, understanding, and emotional safety. When partners communicate with love, clarity, and empathy, they strengthen their bond and build trust and security.

Love is about saying things right and making others feel heard, valued, and cherished. By expressing affection through words, providing reassurance, clearly communicating needs and boundaries, and avoiding misunderstandings, couples can cultivate a relationship that thrives on open, honest, and meaningful conversation.

CHAPTER 7

The Female Social Network: Friendships, Alliances, and Rivalries

*"Friendship is born when one person says to another: 'What!
You too? I thought I was the only one.'"* – C.S. Lewis

Female friendships are intricate, powerful, and profoundly influential in shaping individual experiences and social dynamics. Unlike male friendships, which often center around shared activities, female friendships are typically more emotionally rich and characterized by deep conversations, emotional support, and mutual understanding. These bonds are vital in personal development, emotional well-being, and professional advancement. Yet, like any social network, they are not without their complexities; alliances shift, unspoken rules govern interactions, and rivalries may emerge. Understanding these elements can provide valuable insight into how women navigate social relationships gracefully and resiliently.

Building and Maintaining Friendships

From childhood through adulthood, women form friendships in various ways, ranging from shared experiences in school and workplaces to digital interactions on social media platforms. These friendships often develop through mutual trust, emotional vulnerability, and consistent communication. Unlike transactional relationships, where exchanges are based on utility, female friendships tend to be nurtured through an ongoing exchange of emotional labor and shared experiences.

The Importance of Shared Experiences

Many deep female friendships begin with a moment of shared experience or understanding. These initial moments create a foundation for trust and deeper connection, whether the bond formed over a stressful workplace situation, mutual interests like fitness or books, or a shared cultural background. This is why women often create strong bonds with colleagues, classmates, or other mothers in parenting groups—shared experiences naturally foster emotional intimacy.

Consistency and Reciprocity

Maintaining friendships requires effort. Women often nurture relationships through regular communication—texting, video calls, or in-person meetups. Unlike casual acquaintances, deep friendships thrive on the principle of reciprocity. When one friend consistently initiates plans or provides emotional support without reciprocation, resentment can build over time. This balance of give-and-take is crucial for maintaining long-term relationships.

Emotional Vulnerability and Support

Female friendships are uniquely characterized by emotional depth. Women tend to share their fears, hopes, and dreams with close friends, creating an environment where vulnerability is embraced rather than shunned. This emotional openness fosters trust and cements bonds. It is often why female friendships survive life's major transitions—career changes, motherhood, breakups, and personal reinventions.

The Unspoken Rules of Female Social Groups

Social groups in high school, workplaces, or broader social circles operate under unspoken rules that govern behaviors, expectations, and roles. Understanding these rules can help individuals navigate friendships more effectively.

Inclusivity and Hierarchies

Unlike male social groups, which may function with clear hierarchies, female groups tend to operate more subtly, with shifting dynamics based on trust, shared values, and perceived loyalty. Introducing a new person into a tightly knit group may require an informal "vetting" process, where existing members observe whether the newcomer aligns with their values, humor, and social norms.

Communication Styles

Communication within female social networks is often more nuanced than direct. Subtext, tone, and body language are essential in conveying emotions. A simple "I'm fine" response to a concern may carry multiple layers of meaning, requiring emotional intelligence to interpret correctly. Reading between the lines is often a valued skill within female friendships.

Loyalty and Unspoken Codes

There exists a strong expectation of loyalty among women in friendships. These unspoken codes reinforce trust, whether it's keeping secrets, supporting a friend in social settings, or defending a friend's reputation in their absence. A breach of loyalty, such as gossiping or betraying confidence, can lead to deep fractures within friendships and social groups.

Navigating Group Dynamics and Conflicts

Conflict is an inevitable part of any social network. However, female social conflicts often differ from those of their male counterparts regarding expression and resolution. While male disagreements are sometimes direct and quickly resolved, female conflicts can be more emotionally charged and prolonged due to their relational nature.

Identifying the Root of Conflict

Understanding the underlying cause of a conflict is the first step toward resolution. Familiar sources of tension in female friendships include perceived betrayals, changes in group dynamics (such as one friend becoming closer to another), and unbalanced emotional labor. Often, conflicts are fueled by misunderstandings rather than deliberate harm.

Conflict Resolution Strategies

- **Direct but Compassionate Communication** – Instead of letting tensions fester, open conversations about feelings and expectations can prevent conflicts from escalating.

- **Avoiding the "Triangle Effect"** – One common challenge in female social groups is triangulation, where one friend expresses their grievances about another to a third party instead of addressing the issue directly. This can create misunderstandings and unnecessary drama. Encouraging direct dialogue can prevent this dynamic.

- **Setting Boundaries** – Just as friendships require emotional openness, they also need boundaries. Women should feel empowered to set limits on what they can offer emotionally and mentally in friendships without fear of damaging the relationship.

- **Recognizing When to Walk Away** – Not all friendships are meant to last forever. If a relationship becomes toxic or draining, it is okay to step away without guilt. A graceful exit can sometimes preserve mutual respect.

Recognizing Loyalty, Competition, and Emotional Support in Friendships

Female friendships blend warmth, support, and sometimes unspoken competition. Acknowledging these elements can help women navigate relationships with greater awareness and emotional intelligence.

Loyalty as a Cornerstone

One of the strongest pillars of female friendships is loyalty. Women expect their closest friends to stand by them through challenges, speak highly of them in their absence, and provide emotional sanctuary. Loyalty strengthens bonds, making women feel safe and valued within their friendships.

The Role of Healthy Competition

Contrary to negative stereotypes that depict female friendships as inherently competitive, healthy competition can be a motivating force. Seeing a friend achieve career success, maintain a strong relationship, or accomplish personal goals can inspire others to push themselves. The key difference between healthy and unhealthy competition lies in intent—when competition becomes a means to uplift rather than diminish, it can be a powerful force for growth.

Emotional Support: The Backbone of Female Friendships

Women often rely on each other for deep emotional support, particularly during difficult times. Emotional support fosters trust and security, offering encouragement after a breakup, celebrating a career milestone, or simply listening without judgment. Being emotionally available for a friend without expecting immediate reciprocity is one of the most beautiful aspects of female friendships.

Conclusion

Female social networks are intricate and powerful, offering support, inspiration, and, at times, challenges. Understanding friendship-building mechanisms, the unspoken social rules, group dynamics, and the balance between loyalty and competition can help women confidently navigate their friendships. By fostering open communication, setting healthy boundaries, and recognizing the unique strengths of female friendships, women can cultivate relationships that enrich their lives and stand the test of time.

CHAPTER 8

Thinking Like a Woman: Developing Emotional Awareness

"The great gift of human beings is that we have the power of empathy." – Meryl Streep.

Understanding Her Thought Process: Shifting Your Perspective

One must learn to see the world through her eyes to connect with a woman truly. Women often approach problems, relationships, and emotions differently than men. This isn't due to mere preference but is primarily influenced by social conditioning, brain chemistry, and evolutionary psychology. Women tend to be more attuned to emotional nuances and social dynamics, which means their thought processes incorporate more layers of consideration and complexity.

One of the key aspects of shifting your perspective is recognizing that logic and emotion are not opposing forces but complementary ones. While men may lean towards solving problems with direct action, women often seek validation, emotional processing, and relational context before deciding. This means that instead of focusing solely on offering solutions, it is frequently more valuable to listen, acknowledge feelings, and validate experiences.

The Power of Context in Female Thought Processes

Women are generally more context-oriented in their thinking. They consider past experiences, emotions, and how their decisions affect others. This is why, in many cases, their decision-making process may seem more intricate. They tend to think holistically, meaning that a single conversation is not just about the words exchanged but about tone, body language, and underlying emotions. Recognizing this depth will help communicate more effectively and with greater sensitivity.

The Role of Intuition in Female Decision-Making

Intuition is often described as understanding something instinctively without needing conscious reasoning. While everyone possesses intuition, studies suggest that women are particularly adept at using it. This is partially due to a stronger connection between the brain's left and right hemispheres, simultaneously allowing quicker access to emotional and logical information.

Women's intuition is not mystical but rather an acute awareness of subtle cues, micro expressions, tone changes, and energy shifts. This ability is honed over time due to a heightened focus on social bonds and emotional intelligence.

Recognizing the Signals

Practice tuning into nonverbal cues and emotional undercurrents to think more like a woman and develop emotional awareness. Pay attention to:

- **Facial expressions**: A slight furrow in her brow or hesitation before speaking can indicate an underlying emotion she may not vocalize.

- **The tone of voice**: A shift in pitch or pace often reveals more than words alone.

- **Body language**: Crossed arms, fidgeting, or avoiding eye contact can signal discomfort or unease.

You can better understand her feelings by honing these observational skills, even when she is not explicitly stating them.

Why Empathy Matters in Every Conversation

Empathy is the ability to put yourself in another person's shoes and understand their feelings and perspectives. It is crucial in building trust, deepening relationships, and fostering emotional intimacy.

The Difference Between Sympathy and Empathy

Many people mistake sympathy for empathy, but the two are distinct. Sympathy is feeling for someone—acknowledging their pain from a distance. On the other hand, empathy is feeling with someone—immersing yourself in their emotions to understand them truly.

To cultivate empathy:

1. **Listen actively** – Instead of thinking about what you will say next, focus entirely on her expression.

2. **Validate emotions** – You don't have to agree with everything she says, but acknowledging her feelings as valid can go a long way.

3. **Ask meaningful questions** – Instead of jumping to solutions, ask, "How did that make you feel?" or "What do you need right now?"

4. **Practice perspective-taking** – Imagine how you would feel if you were in her position.

When empathy becomes a core part of your communication, it transforms the dynamic of any relationship. Women tend to feel more comfortable and emotionally safe with individuals who demonstrate genuine empathy, making interactions more meaningful and fulfilling.

Anticipating Her Needs and Emotions

Understanding and anticipating a woman's emotional needs requires emotional intelligence, patience, and attentiveness. It is not about mind-reading but about being present and observant in the relationship.

The Importance of Emotional Responsiveness

Women value emotional responsiveness, meaning they appreciate when their emotions are acknowledged and respected. This means recognizing when she needs comfort, space, encouragement, or someone to listen without judgment.

Here are some ways to develop this ability:

- **Pay attention to patterns** – If she seems quieter than usual after work, this could indicate stress. If she withdraws after an argument, she may need reassurance before engaging in further discussion.

- **Check-in regularly** – Simple questions like, "How are you feeling today?" or "Is there anything on your mind?" can show that you care.

- **Be proactive** – Instead of waiting for her to voice a need, anticipate it. If she's had a long day, offering to take care of small tasks can be a thoughtful gesture.

The Balance Between Emotional Awareness and Personal Boundaries

While emotional awareness is a powerful tool in relationships, it is equally essential to maintain healthy boundaries. Being in tune with someone's emotions does not mean absorbing them completely. Emotional support should be a two-way street where both individuals feel heard and valued.

Final Thoughts

Thinking like a woman doesn't mean abandoning your thinking; it means expanding your perspective to incorporate emotional depth, intuition, and empathy. Women value connection, understanding, and the feeling of being indeed heard. Developing emotional awareness enhances your interactions with women and overall emotional intelligence, making you more perceptive, compassionate, and well-rounded.

"When you show deep empathy toward others, their defensive energy decreases, and positive energy replaces it. That's when you can get more creative in solving problems." – Stephen Covey.

CHAPTER 9

The Keys to a Lasting Connection

"The meeting of two personalities is like the contact of two chemical substances: if there is any reaction, both are transformed." — Carl Jung.

Keeping Conversations Engaging and Emotionally Fulfilling

One of the most significant factors in maintaining a deep and lasting connection is the quality of your conversations. While many relationships start with an effortless flow of words, sustaining engaging and emotionally enriching dialogues over time requires intentional effort.

Active listening is the cornerstone of meaningful conversations. Instead of waiting for your turn to speak, practice truly hearing what she says, acknowledging her emotions, and responding in a way that shows you understand and value her perspective. Reflective listening, paraphrasing, or summarizing her words, can reinforce your engagement.

Beyond listening, asking thoughtful and open-ended questions fosters deeper discussions. Instead of "How was your day?" try "What was the most interesting part of your day?" or "What's something that made you smile today?" These questions invite more than routine answers; they allow for storytelling, laughter, and meaningful emotional exchange.

Maintaining a balance between sharing and inquiring is crucial to keeping conversations vibrant. A relationship is a two-way street, and vulnerability is an essential ingredient. Opening up about your feelings, aspirations, and experiences creates a safe space for her to do the same.

Additionally, bringing curiosity into everyday talks can add excitement. Discuss dreams, passions, or hypothetical scenarios, like "If we could live anywhere in the world for a year, where would it be and why?" Such playful yet thought-provoking exchanges keep the relationship dynamic and prevent conversations from becoming routine or transactional.

The Importance of Consistency and Reliability in Communication

Reliability in communication is one of the strongest pillars of trust in any relationship. A lasting connection requires a foundation where both partners feel secure in each other's emotional availability and responsiveness.

Consistency in communication does not mean constant interaction but rather predictability in emotional support. If you say you will call, follow through. If she expresses concerns, acknowledge them and make her feel heard. These seemingly small actions accumulate over time, building a strong sense of security and trust.

Reliability extends beyond responding to texts or calls; it includes emotional consistency. Sudden shifts from warm and engaged to distant and unresponsive can create confusion and insecurity. While everyone needs space, explaining your feelings such as, "I'm feeling a little overwhelmed today, but I just need some time to recharge"—helps maintain emotional stability within the relationship.

Honoring commitments in communication also fosters a sense of safety. If you establish traditions like a weekly check-in to discuss feelings, goals, or concerns, keeping those moments sacred reinforces the depth of your bond.

Recognizing and Reinforcing Emotional Intimacy Over Time

Emotional intimacy does not form overnight; it is cultivated through shared experiences, deep conversations, and mutual understanding. One of the keys to maintaining this level of closeness is recognizing and appreciating it.

Gratitude is a powerful tool in reinforcing emotional intimacy. A simple "I appreciate you for..." or "I love how you always..." can go a long way in making her feel valued. Noticing and vocalizing the little things; whether it's how she comforts you when you're stressed or how she lights up when talking about something she loves, deepens the emotional connection.

Creating meaningful rituals also strengthens intimacy. Whether it's a morning text, a weekly date night, or a shared hobby, these small yet significant gestures develop a sense of continuity and emotional reinforcement.

Another key to maintaining emotional closeness is addressing conflicts with care. Disagreements are inevitable, but how they are handled determines the strength of your connection. Approaching conflict with an open heart, focusing on resolution rather than blame, and maintaining a respectful tone preserve emotional closeness even in difficult moments.

Additionally, fostering emotional intimacy means being present. In a world full of distractions, consciously focusing solely on her during quality time, putting away your phone, making eye contact, and being mentally engaged, demonstrates your commitment to the relationship.

How to Evolve with Her as the Relationship Grows

A relationship is a living entity, constantly evolving as individuals change and grow. The key to sustaining a lasting connection is embracing and adapting to these changes rather than resisting them.

Personal growth is inevitable, and it's important to celebrate each other's journeys. Encouraging her dreams, supporting her ambitions, and respecting how she evolves strengthen the foundation of your bond. At the same time, sharing your personal growth and aspirations keeps the relationship mutually inspiring.

Flexibility is essential when navigating changes. The dynamics of a relationship may shift due to career developments, personal challenges, or new life experiences. Instead of fearing these transitions, view them as opportunities to deepen your understanding of each other. Discuss your evolving needs, desires, and perspectives openly to ensure you're growing in alignment rather than drifting apart.

Keeping a sense of adventure alive in the relationship also fosters continued growth. Trying new activities together, travelling to new places, or even learning new skills as a couple creates shared experiences that strengthen your bond.

Lastly, revisiting your relationship's core values and long-term vision helps maintain alignment. Periodically checking in on each other's dreams, priorities, and expectations ensures that both partners remain connected and adaptable to the ever-changing nature of life and love.

Final Thoughts

A lasting connection is not about perfection but effort, presence, and a willingness to evolve together. You cultivate a relationship that stands the test of time by keeping conversations engaging, consistent and reliable in communication, reinforcing emotional intimacy, and embracing growth. Genuine connection is built in the small moments, through laughter, deep conversations, thoughtful gestures, and unwavering support. In nurturing these elements, you create a bond that lasts and thrives.

CHAPTER 10

Mastering the Art of Female Communication

"Women speak two languages—one of which is verbal." – William Shakespeare (A reminder that body language and emotions are part of the conversation, too.)

Understanding the Fundamentals

Communication is the foundation of every professional, romantic, or social relationship. While much of communication is universal, understanding the nuances of female communication requires emotional intelligence and adaptability beyond simple conversation. Women generally tend to communicate more on emotional context, active listening, and subtle nonverbal cues. This chapter delves into how to master female communication, ensuring that interactions are practical but also meaningful and authentic.

Practical Techniques to Apply in Daily Interactions

1. Active Listening and Emotional Validation

Women often communicate to express emotions and build connections rather than merely exchange information. Practicing active listening means fully engaging with what is being said and responding in a way that makes the speaker feel heard and understood. To do this effectively:

- Maintain eye contact and nod occasionally to show attentiveness.

- Paraphrase or summarize what has been said to confirm understanding.

- Validate emotions by acknowledging feelings instead of dismissing them.

- Avoid rushing to solve a problem unless explicitly asked for advice.

2. Mirroring and Matching Communication Styles

Adapting your communication style to mirror the other person can enhance connection. This doesn't mean mimicking but instead adjusting the tone, pace, and energy level to create rapport. Matching that energy fosters a sense of comfort and understanding if someone speaks softly and reflectively.

3. Reading Between the Lines

Many women communicate through implication and subtle cues rather than direct statements. Pay attention to nonverbal signs such as body language, facial expressions, and tone of voice. For instance:

- A pause before answering may indicate hesitation or deeper emotions.

- A slight change in tone could suggest discomfort or excitement.

- Crossed arms might signal defensiveness while leaning in, which could suggest engagement.

4. Using Open-Ended Questions

Encouraging deeper conversations requires open-ended questions that invite thoughtful responses rather than one-word answers. Instead of asking, "Did you have a good day?" try "What was the highlight of your day?" This approach fosters more meaningful dialogue and helps build emotional intimacy.

5. Balancing Assertiveness with Sensitivity

Confidence is key in communication but must be paired with emotional awareness. Being assertive without aggression ensures that your opinions are heard while respecting the other person's perspective. This balance can be achieved by:

- Using "I" statements to express thoughts without sounding accusatory (e.g., "I feel that..." instead of "You always...").

- Expressing appreciation and gratitude within the conversation.

- Maintaining a respectful and non-confrontational tone.

How to Maintain Authenticity While Adapting Your Approach

Adapting to different communication styles does not mean losing authenticity. The key is to remain true to your values while being flexible in expressing yourself.

1. Know Your Core Values

Before adjusting your communication approach, be clear on your core values. Authenticity stems from knowing what you stand for and ensuring your interactions align with these principles.

2. Be Honest Yet Tactful

Honesty is vital, but delivery matters. Women often appreciate honesty wrapped in empathy. Instead of saying, "That idea won't work," consider, "I see where you're coming from; have you thought about this alternative?"

3. Use Your Unique Voice

Your personal communication style is part of your identity. While adapting to different situations is beneficial, forcing yourself into an unnatural style can make interactions feel inauthentic. Strive for a balance where adaptation enhances your expression rather than replaces it.

4. Practice Self-Awareness

Regularly reflecting on how you communicate can help identify areas for growth while ensuring that you remain true to yourself. Pay attention to patterns in your interactions and adjust as necessary without compromising your authenticity.

Overcoming Communication Barriers in Different Life Stages

Life experiences shape communication styles. Understanding how different life stages affect communication helps in forming more profound connections.

1. Teenage and Early Adulthood Communication

- Often marked by heightened emotions and self-discovery.

- Be patient, listen actively, and provide reassurance.

- Offer guidance without imposing opinions.

2. Midlife and Career-Focused Communication

- Balances personal and professional responsibilities.

- Be concise, respectful of time, and supportive.

- Encourage challenges and accomplishments.

3. Later Life Communication

- Often values reminiscing, wisdom-sharing, and emotional connection.

- Engage in storytelling and show genuine interest in experiences.

- Use patience and presence to create meaningful moments.

Final Insights on Fostering Deeper, More Meaningful Relationships

Effective communication with women is not about adhering to rigid rules but about developing emotional intelligence, patience, and respect. Key takeaways include:

- **Listen to understand, not just to respond.**

- **Adapt without losing authenticity.**

- **Recognize that emotions play a significant role in communication.**

- **Create a safe space for open, honest dialogue.**

Applying these principles will enhance your ability to connect deeper, fostering relationships built on trust, respect, and mutual understanding. Communication is an art that, when mastered, transforms how we relate to others in profound and fulfilling ways.

CHAPTER 11

Building and Sustaining Female Friendships

The Anatomy of Female Friendships

Female friendships are often described as lifelines, soul-sister bonds, or unspoken contracts of emotional loyalty and there's a reason for that. Unlike many male friendships, which may orbit around shared activities, many female friendships go deeper into emotional intimacy, shared vulnerability, and mutual caretaking. These are not merely social connections; they're emotional ecosystems.

At the core of these relationships lies a profound social bonding, often fueled by **shared vulnerability** and **mutual support**. In those long phone calls, quiet check-ins, unexpected texts on a hard day, and remembering small details like a challenging presentation at work or a yearly health checkup; the glue of female friendship sets. This isn't about being constantly present; it's about being emotionally available.

What's fascinating is that the emotional closeness in female friendships isn't just cultural; it's **biological**. Neuroscience gives us an incredible window into this. You've probably heard of the "fight or flight" response; how the body responds to stress. But for women, researchers have identified a parallel stress response called **"tend and befriend."** Coined by psychologist Shelley Taylor, this theory proposes that under stress, women are biologically wired to seek social support and care for others, especially in close relationships. Oxytocin—the so-called "bonding hormone"—stars in this response, encouraging affiliation rather than aggression.

This doesn't mean men don't seek connection, but the patterns differ. Women connect by **discussing feelings**, sharing their internal experiences, and seeking mutual understanding. Female friendships are often built on **emotional resonance**, not just shared interests. It's the feeling of "you get me;" of being seen and accepted not just for what you do but for who you are.

Friendships between women often develop through **emotional mirroring**. One shares something vulnerable, the other mirrors that vulnerability, perhaps with a similar story or a validating response. These reciprocal exchanges build emotional trust, the bedrock of long-lasting bonds.

There's also a cultural layer to this. Women are frequently socialized to be relational, valuing empathy, connection, and community. While this isn't universally true across all cultures, it's a pattern seen in many. Girls are encouraged to nurture, care, and resolve conflict verbally from a young age. These early scripts carry over into adult friendships.

However, female friendships are not immune to challenges. Their depth can make them feel intense, sometimes even overwhelming. And just like romantic relationships, they can have their ups and downs, requiring care, maintenance, and growth. The remaining sections of this chapter dive into how women build these friendships in adulthood, what makes them thrive, the roles we play in them, and how we keep them strong across the changing seasons of life.

11.2 Making Female Friends as an Adult

Let's be honest: making friends as an adult is awkward. Unlike childhood or college, where you're thrown into shared spaces with built-in icebreakers, adult life doesn't offer as many organic opportunities to meet new people. Add in the social anxiety that many people experience and the intimidation of approaching a potential friend and it's no wonder so many adult women feel isolated despite wanting a connection.

The first hurdle is often **internal resistance**. "What if she thinks I'm weird?" "What if she already has enough friends?" "What if I say the wrong thing?" These mental roadblocks can paralyze us before we've even tried. The key to breaking through is recognizing that most people are open to friendship but don't know how to signal it.

This is where **small, repeated exposure** becomes magic. You don't have to deliver a TED Talk to become someone's friend, you need a few casual, low-stakes interactions. Think: the neighbor you wave to, the coworker you chat with in the break room, or the fellow dog parent at the park. These repeated interactions often called "mere exposure" in psychology, build familiarity, which breeds comfort.

Next comes **trust signaling**. In a world where everyone manages busy schedules, skepticism, and emotional baggage, subtle trust cues go a long way. It might be showing up consistently, remembering someone's name, or making a thoughtful comment like, "I noticed you seemed a little off the other day, are you okay?" These small gestures signal reliability and care; two things we unconsciously scan for when deciding who feels safe.

Now, when the time comes to open up, the biggest pitfall is oversharing too fast. Vulnerability is powerful, but it should be mutual and gradual. Share a little, observe the response, and then go more profound if it feels right. Dumping your life story in one sitting can feel more like an emotional hijack than a bonding moment. Trust builds in layers, like sediment forming over time, not all at once.

Also, don't underestimate the value of **intentionality**. If you meet someone your vibe with, suggest a low-key hangout: "Want to grab coffee sometime?" or "I'd love to hear more about that project, let's chat over lunch." Yes, it might feel scary to initiate. But remember, adults are busy; not disinterested. Sometimes, all it takes is someone willing to go first.

11.3 The Secret to Deep Female Friendships: Emotional Reciprocity

If a single ingredient transforms a friendship from casual to soul-deep, it's **emotional reciprocity**. This is the give-and-take, the showing up and being shown up for, the checking in and being checked on. It's how trust grows, how connection deepens, and how friendships withstand the tests of time.

You can think of emotional reciprocity as an **emotional bank account**. Every kind gesture, every moment of listening, every memory remembered, or affirmation given; these are deposits. Conversely, forgetting meaningful things, showing up inconsistently, or taking more than you give can feel like withdrawals. And just like with money, the friendship becomes emotionally bankrupt if there are too many withdrawals without enough deposits.

Now, this doesn't mean we should treat our friendships like spreadsheets. It's not about keeping scores. It's about **balance;** a shared sense of being emotionally nourished. Healthy friendships have a rhythm. Sometimes, one person gives more, especially during a hard season, and then that dynamic shifts naturally over time.

The best friendships are built on **sharing, listening, and remembering**. Sharing helps us feel seen. Listening allows the other person to feel valued. And remembering? That's the secret sauce. When someone recalls a story you told a month ago or asks how your mom is doing after you mentioned her health scare in passing; that's where the magic lives. It communicates: *You matter. I'm invested.*

But here's where many women get stuck—**one-sided friendships**. Maybe you've been the emotional support line for someone who rarely asks how *you* are. Perhaps you've consistently shown up for coffee, birthdays, or crises but feel a kind of emptiness when you need the same in return. It's easy to fall into a caretaker role, especially if you're wired for empathy or have a "fix-it" personality.

The challenge is recognizing when you're over-giving out of obligation or fear of conflict. Ask yourself: *Does this friendship leave me feeling fulfilled or depleted? Do I feel emotionally safe being myself? Is there room for my needs, too?* If the answer is consistently no, it may be time to set boundaries—or even reevaluate the role of that friendship in your life.

Remember: reciprocity isn't just about giving the same thing. It's about giving what each person needs. Maybe one friend needs verbal reassurance, while another thrives on shared experiences. The key is *attunement*—being responsive to the unique emotional language of each relationship.

11.4 Friendship Styles Among Women

Just like in romantic relationships, we all have different **styles** of friendship. Understanding your style and that of the women around you can help reduce misunderstandings, prevent hurt feelings, and strengthen your bonds.

Let's look at three typical friendship roles:

The Nurturer

She's the caretaker, the check-in queen, the one who always brings a snack and remembers birthdays. Nurturers are often intuitive, emotionally generous, and great listeners. They can sense when something's off and offer quiet support without being asked.

Challenges: Sometimes, Nurturers overextend themselves, forgetting to ask for help in return. They may feel unappreciated or emotionally drained if their efforts aren't reciprocated.

The Connector

She's the social butterfly, the planner, the one who gathers everyone for brunch or a birthday surprise. Connectors build bridges between people, create community, and often have a vast network of friends.

Challenges: Connectors may spread themselves too thin or feel unappreciated when others don't use the same organizing energy. They might struggle to go deep in one-on-one dynamics if they always manage group energy.

The Protector

She's fiercely loyal, no-nonsense, and the first to say, "You don't deserve to be treated like that." Protectors are the ones you call when you need backup or a reality check. They have your back, even when it's hard.

Challenges: Protectors can sometimes be perceived as harsh or guarded, especially if they don't easily show vulnerability. They may struggle with softness, especially in friendships where emotional expression is key.

Here's the fun part: **you probably aren't just one** of these. You might be a Nurturer with your childhood friends, a Connector at work, and a Protector in your family. These styles can shift based on the relationship, life stage, or emotional context.

Understanding **introverted vs. extroverted** friendship styles also helps. Extroverts may crave regular contact and group hangouts, while introverts prefer deep one-on-one conversations and longer stretches between check-ins. Misunderstandings often happen when styles don't align, like when an extroverted friend thinks an introvert is pulling away or an introvert feels overwhelmed by too many social plans.

The solution? **Clarity and compassion**. Talk about your needs. Ask others about theirs. There's no "right" way to be a friend; just a willingness to understand and adapt.

11.5 Group Dynamics vs. One-on-One Friendships

Female friendship groups can feel like mini ecosystems; vibrant, comforting, sometimes dramatic, and often profoundly formative. A special joy comes from laughing with three or four women who know your history, cheer you on, and call you out with equal love. But navigating group dynamics can also be...tricky.

Let's talk about **friendship triangles** first. These happen when three friends are all connected but not always equally. Maybe two are closer, and the third feels left out. Or one person always seems to be the go-between. These dynamics can stir up insecurity, jealousy, or exclusion, even when no one means harm.

The key is to **communicate openly** and avoid secrecy. If two people hang out, there's no need to hide it—but be sensitive to how it might land. Simple reassurances like, "We missed you!"

or "Let's plan something soon, all three of us," go a long way. If you feel left out, it's okay to speak up. "Hey, I've been feeling a little on the edge lately. I miss our group vibe."

Group friendships can also be both **empowering and draining**. On the one hand, they offer laughter, variety, and shared memories. On the other hand, they can come with **hidden hierarchies**, unspoken loyalties, and an unspoken fear of rocking the boat. Sometimes, the group takes on a vibe—maybe sarcasm-heavy or emotionally avoidant—that doesn't work for everyone, but no one knows how to shift it.

One-on-one friendships are often more emotionally safe because they don't involve **performing** for a group. They allow for more profound vulnerability, fewer social dynamics, and usually a more relaxed, customized bond. You don't have to be "on." You can just be.

There's no need to choose one over the other. The healthiest friendship circles allow for fluidity—moments where the group gathers and moments where individual friendships deepen privately. The goal is to foster an environment where everyone feels included and seen, whether in the crowd or the quiet.

11.6 Maintaining Long-Term Female Friendships

When you've been friends with someone for five, ten, or even twenty years, your bond is no longer just a friendship—it's a shared history. You've become part of each other's timeline. You remember her awkward high school phase, the ex she thought she'd marry, the job she almost didn't take. She remembers your grief after your dad died, the time you dyed your hair pink to feel something, and the way you stood up for yourself after years of people-pleasing.

But longevity doesn't guarantee closeness. Just because a friendship has years under its belt doesn't mean it's healthy or growing. Like any long-term relationship, female friendships need maintenance, evolution, and, sometimes, repair.

Rituals, Check-ins, and Memory-Making

One of the most grounding aspects of long-term friendships is the rituals you build together. Maybe it's Friday night wine dates, annual birthday dinners, holiday cookie baking, or Sunday morning walks. These aren't just routines—they're emotional touchpoints that tether you to each other's lives.

Even if you don't see each other weekly or monthly, **intentional check-ins** help sustain the bond. A simple "Thinking of you, how are you doing?" can mean more than a grand gesture. Technology helps here; voice notes, memes, quick texts that say, "This reminded me of you." It's less about how *often* you talk and more about how *meaningfully* you stay connected.

Long-term friends are also **memory-keepers**. They remind you of who you were and who you're becoming. They hold your stories, and you have theirs. Lean into that. Revisit shared memories with warmth but also make new ones. Plan a trip together. Start a shared playlist. Try a book club, even if it's just the two of you. Nostalgia is beautiful—but growing new roots matters, too.

Conflict Resolution Tips Specific to Female Friendships

Let's get real: even the most potent female friendships will face conflict. It might be subtle (an ignored text, a cancelled plan that stung) or seismic (a betrayal, a boundary crossed, a buildup of resentment).

One reason conflict can feel incredibly intense in female friendships is that these relationships are often emotionally deep. We expect our friends to understand, validate, and prioritize us. So, when something feels off, the disappointment hits harder.

Here are a few principles to keep in your emotional toolbox:

- **Don't let the silence grow mold.** Avoidance rarely resolves tension; it just buries it under layers of awkwardness. If something's bothering you, bring it up with curiosity, not accusation. Try: "Hey, I noticed we've been a little distant lately, can we talk?"

- **Use "I" language.** Instead of "You never support me," try "I felt alone when I was going through that, and I needed you." It invites empathy instead of defensiveness.

- **Stay rooted in the goal.** The goal isn't to be right; it's to reconnect. Ask yourself, "What do I want from this conversation? 1More understanding? Clarity? Repair?"

- **Own your part.** Rarely is conflict one-sided. Even if you're mainly in the right, acknowledge where you could've handled something better. Accountability builds trust.

And remember: some friendships bounce back stronger after conflict Others naturally fade or require a new kind of boundary. Not all long-term friendships are meant to last forever in the same way. But many can evolve—if both people are willing.

How to Grow Together Through Life Transitions

One of the biggest challenges in sustaining long-term female friendships is simply this: **life changes**. You're not the same person you were five years ago and neither is she. Careers shift. People move. Kids come into the picture. Divorce happens. Faith evolves. Energy levels change. Priorities realign.

It's easy to drift apart during these seasons—not out of malice, but out of logistics. The friend who used to be your go-to weekend partner might now juggle three kids and a demanding job. Or maybe *you're* the one who feels spread thin, barely holding together your schedule.

The key to maintaining friendship through transitions is **grace**, grace for each other's realities and limitations. It means not taking things personally when a friend is slow to respond or has less emotional bandwidth than before. It also means not ghosting just because life gets busy.

Instead, stay honest. Say, "Hey, I know we haven't connected much, I miss you. Can we find a new rhythm that works for both of us?" It might be less frequent phone calls. It might be one intentional dinner every two months. The frequency matters less than the intention behind it.

And don't underestimate the power of **re-introducing yourselves**. Sometimes, after years of friendship, we assume we know each other—but people change. Ask more profound questions again. "What's been on your heart lately?" "How do you want to be supported right now?" These check-ins keep the friendship alive not just based on who you were, but who you are becoming.

Wrapping It All Together: Female Friendships Are Living, Breathing Things

If there's one truth about female friendship, it's this: they're **living, breathing relationships** that require intention, honesty, and care. They are not passive; they don't thrive on autopilot. But when nurtured, they become one of our most life-giving sources of joy, grounding, and strength.

Nicci Brochard & Dr.Ben Chuba

Female friendships teach us to be vulnerable, listen, love without expectation, and hold space for another person's truth. They challenge us to grow. They remind us we are not alone.

So, whether you're trying to make new friends, deepen existing bonds, or revive a relationship that's gone quietly, remember this: friendship doesn't have to be perfect to be powerful. It just has to be authentic.

CHAPTER 12

Navigating and Managing Complexities in Women's Social Circles

Female friendships are some of the most emotionally fulfilling relationships we can have. They offer support, empathy, shared understanding, and a sense of community that is often hard to replicate. But like any relationship, they come with layers, nuanced expectations, evolving boundaries, and the occasional emotional minefield. In this chapter, we will unpack the complexities that can arise in women's social circles and explore practical, heartfelt ways to navigate them with grace and honesty.

12.1 The Unspoken Rules of Female Friendship

Every social circle has a rhythm and unspoken code governing how people interact, show support, or disagree. In female friendships, these unwritten rules can be subtle but powerful.

Code-switching, loyalty, and unspoken obligations

Women often shift their language, tone, or demeanor depending on who they're around—a practice known as code-switching. In friendship circles, this might mean playing peacemaker with one friend while being the truth-teller with another. It's not always about being inauthentic; sometimes, it's about adjusting to protect harmony. However, too much code-switching can leave you feeling like you're walking on eggshells.

Loyalty is another unspoken rule, expecting to take sides, keep confidences, or show up emotionally even when your tank is empty. These obligations are rarely discussed outright but can feel very real.

The importance of tone, inclusion, and subtle gestures

In women's friendships, tone is everything. A simple "I'm fine" can mean different things depending on the delivery. The weight of a raised eyebrow, a pause in a group chat, or being left out of a plan can speak volumes. These small moments build up either reinforcing trust or quietly eroding it. Inclusion is sacred in many women's circles. Being invited signals that you matter even if you can't attend. It's not about perfection; it's about presence.

The emotional contract behind female friendship

Many women enter friendships with an emotional contract that includes empathy, mutual support, and consistent emotional availability. These contracts aren't written down, but you feel it when they're broken. For instance, if you're always calling, supporting, or forgiving, and your friend never returns the emotional favor, that imbalance becomes heavy. Understanding that an unspoken emotional contract is often at play can help you become more intentional in giving and receiving support.

12.2 Common Challenges and How to Overcome Them

Let's face it: even the most beautiful friendships aren't immune to friction. Here's how to navigate some of the more common hurdles.

Jealousy, comparison, and social competition

It's easy to feel jealous when your friend gets that dream job, finds a great partner, or reaches a milestone you've been working toward. Social comparison is usual but left unchecked, it can become corrosive. The key is awareness. Acknowledge the feeling without judgment. Remind yourself that someone else's success doesn't dim your own. Turning envy into admiration or curiosity can strengthen the friendship. Ask questions, celebrate her win, and share your own goals vulnerably.

Ghosting, slow fades, and unspoken rifts

Sometimes, friendships don't end with a fight—they dissolve silently. A slow fade might come from mismatched priorities, life transitions, or emotional exhaustion. On the other hand, ghosting is more abrupt and often leaves one confused and hurt. Compassion is key if you find yourself on either side of this equation. If you're the one fading out, consider a gentle explanation. If you've been ghosted, resist the urge to obsess over your wrongdoings. Sometimes, the silence says more about them than it does about you.

How to address issues without escalating drama

Addressing conflict in female friendships can feel risky—especially if the fear of drama looms large. But sweeping issues under the rug only creates tension. Approach with curiosity, not accusation. Use "I" statements: "I felt hurt when I wasn't invited" instead of "You excluded me." Stay grounded in your intention: to understand and reconnect, not to win. Timing matters too—avoid confronting someone mid-chaos. A calm moment leads to better outcomes.

12.4 Emotional Labor in Female Friendships

Women are often socialized to be caregivers, emotionally available, nurturing, and attuned to others' needs. But in friendships, this can turn into emotional labor that's unevenly distributed.

Recognizing when one person is carrying the friendship

You may carry more than your share if you continuously check in, remember birthdays, mediate conflicts, and make plans. Emotional labor becomes unsustainable when it's not reciprocated. Pay attention to patterns. Are you always the "therapist friend"? Do your needs get airtime, or are they consistently pushed aside? Friendship should feel like a dance, not a one-person performance.

How to establish mutual support and healthy boundaries

The antidote to imbalanced emotional labor is honest conversation and more precise boundaries. It's okay to say, "I love being here for you, but I also need space to process my stuff." Normalize asking for support, not just offering it. Mutual friendships are built on a rhythm of give and take. Boundaries aren't walls; they're bridges that help relationships thrive without burning you out.

12.5 Managing Transitions and Distance

Life consists of transitions, moves, marriages, babies, career changes. These can strain even the closest bonds.

Navigating life changes without losing the friendship

When your friend's life shifts dramatically, it can be hard to find common ground. Maybe she's suddenly a mom, and you're not, or she's deep into a new relationship, and you're feeling left behind. The key here is flexibility. Accept that the friendship might look different for a while. Check-in without demanding full access. Respect new priorities but hold space for reconnection. Sometimes, simply saying "I miss you" opens the door.

Long-distance friendship dynamics: staying close emotionally

Physical distance doesn't have to mean emotional distance. But staying connected takes intentionality. Don't rely only on Instagram likes or birthday texts. Schedule catch-up calls, send voice notes, or mail something handwritten. Even quick "thinking of you" messages go a long way. It's less about the frequency and more about the consistency of your presence.

12.6 Ending a Female Friendship Gracefully

Not all friendships are meant to last forever, and that's okay. Sometimes, letting go is the healthiest thing you can do.

Signs that a friendship may be toxic or no longer aligned

Pay attention to how you feel after spending time with someone. Do you feel drained, judged, or anxious? Are your boundaries constantly violated? Is there a pattern of one-sidedness, manipulation, or passive-aggressive behavior? A friendship doesn't have to be explosive to be unhealthy. Sometimes, it's no longer aligned with who you are or want to become.

How to create closure with compassion

Ending a friendship doesn't have to be cruel. If the friendship mattered, consider a conversation: "I've valued our time, but I feel we're growing in different directions." A heartfelt message or quiet fade might be necessary if a talk isn't safe or possible. Closure is for you, not necessarily a mutual agreement. Grieve the good parts and honor the role the friendship played.

Avoiding guilt and social backlash

Women are often taught to prioritize harmony and fear being seen as "mean" or "difficult." But ending a friendship isn't inherently cruel; it's frequently courageous. Guilt is natural, but it doesn't mean you made the wrong choice. Focus on the truth of your experience. If mutual friends question your decision, hold your boundaries gently but firmly. You're allowed to choose peace over performance.

12.7 Healing from Friendship Wounds and Rebuilding Trust

Some of the most profound emotional wounds come not from romantic relationships but from female friends. Healing is possible but it takes time and intention.

Processing hurt from female friends: betrayal, abandonment, exclusion

When a friend betrays you, leaves you during a hard time, or excludes you from something meaningful, it can shake your trust. Start by naming the pain. Don't minimize it or try to "move on" too fast. Journal about it. Talk to someone who gets it. Permit yourself to grieve.

Self-reflection vs. blame

Healing isn't about assigning 100% of the blame. It's about understanding what happened, what patterns were at play, and how you want to grow from it. Ask yourself: Did I ignore red 2flags? Was I afraid to speak up? Was I projecting old wounds? Reflection doesn't mean taking all the blame but reclaiming your power.

Rebuilding trust if reconciliation is possible

Not all broken friendships are meant to be revived—but some are. If you both feel there's something worth salvaging, start slow. Acknowledge what happened, apologize if needed, and express what you need moving forward. Rebuilding trust isn't about going back to how things were; it's about creating something new that's more honest.

Learning to be vulnerable again after loss

Friendship wounds can make you guarded. But shutting down only leads to loneliness. Vulnerability is a muscle. Start small. Let someone new in gradually. Share a bit of your story. Ask for help. Trust again—not because people are perfect, but because you're worthy of connection.

In the end, female friendships are sacred terrain. They shape how we see ourselves, grow, and find joy in the everyday. Navigating the complexities doesn't mean avoiding conflict or staying surface-level. It means showing up with honesty, tenderness, and a commitment to keep learning. The most fulfilling friendships are the ones where you can be fully yourself and still be deeply loved.

CHAPTER 13

10 Things Women Discuss About Men and Why They Do

L et's be honest; when women get together, the conversation can go from brunch plans to deep life philosophies within minutes. But one recurring topic that never seems to go out of style? Men. Whether swooning, venting, analyzing, or laughing, men make their way into the chat for various reasons. Here are ten of the most common things women talk about when it comes to men, with a look at the psychology, the sisterhood, the hilarity, and the heart behind each one.

1. Emotional Availability (or Lack Thereof)

Why Women Talk About It: Because feelings matter and trying to understand someone who doesn't openly express theirs can feel like decoding ancient hieroglyphics.

The Conversation: "Why won't he just tell me how he feels?" "He said he's fine, but his vibe is off."

Anecdote: Tasha once dated a guy who replied "k" whenever she asked him something meaningful. After a month of emotional detective work, she finally told him, "I can't be in a relationship with a wall."

Fun Fact: Studies have shown that women, on average, are more verbally expressive than men, which can lead to a mismatch in communication styles.

2. Communication Habits

Why Women Talk About It: A lot can ride on a text (or the lack of one).

The Conversation: "He left me on read for 8 hours. Is he ghosting me or just busy?" "His texts went from novels to one-liners. What does it mean?"

Anecdote: Sara screenshots a guy's messages and sends them to the group chat, complete with emoji commentary. Her friends replied, "This screams 'slow fade.' Bail."

Fun Fact: According to Pew Research, nearly 31% of adults have ghosted someone, but women are more likely to talk about being ghosted than men.

3. Physical Attraction and Chemistry

Why Women Talk About It: That first spark matters, and chemistry can be both exhilarating and confusing.

The Conversation: "He smells *so* good. Like, dangerously good." "The way he looked at me across the table... whew!"

Anecdote: Jen once texted her best friend from the bathroom during a first date: "If he smiles at me like that one more time, I might just marry him."

Fun Fact: Pheromones and scent play a more significant role in attraction than most people realize; it's science, not just hormones.

4. Mixed Signals

Why Women Talk About It: Because deciphering them is like trying to solve a riddle wrapped in a mystery inside a brooding Instagram DM.

The Conversation: "He said he's not ready for a relationship but also wants to cuddle?" "He flirts, then ghosts. What gives?"

Anecdote: Emily dubbed one guy "Captain Contradiction" after he introduced her to his parents, then said he "wasn't looking for anything serious."

Fun Fact: Ambiguity keeps people hooked. The "uncertainty effect" shows that we become more interested in people with unclear feelings.

5. Effort and Thoughtfulness

Why Women Talk About It: Because effort is often equated with care, it's a big deal when someone *shows up* emotionally and mentally.

The Conversation: "He remembered I had a meeting today and sent a 'good luck' text." "He planned a whole picnic—with my favorite wine!"

Anecdote: Nina cried (the good kind) when her boyfriend brought her soup, tissues, and a playlist titled "Healing Vibes" while she was sick.

Fun Fact: Small gestures trigger oxytocin, the "bonding hormone," which makes people feel closer.

6. Red Flags

Why Women Talk About It: Sometimes, it takes a friend to point out the red flag you've been painting green.

The Conversation: "He says all his exes are 'crazy.' That's a red flag, right?" "He still texts his ex... like a lot."

Anecdote: Maya kept brushing off the fact that her guy would only call her at night. Her friends staged a "Red Flag Intervention" with literal red flags from the dollar store.

Fun Fact: One of the top red flags identified by women is emotional manipulation, followed closely by a lack of accountability.

7. Green Flags

Why Women Talk About It: Because noticing healthy traits deserves just as much airtime as red flags—maybe even more.

The Conversation: "He asked me how he could support me better. I almost passed out." "He respects boundaries without making it weird—10/10."

Anecdote: After several questionable dates, Rachel gushed about a guy who brought her tea, listened intently, and walked her to her car. Her friend texted later: "This one sounds like a golden retriever in human form. Keep him."

Fun Fact: Traits like emotional intelligence and empathy are desirable in long-term partners.

8. The "Situationship" Dilemma

Why Women Talk About It: Because undefined relationships are confusing, women often need to process what they want versus what they're settling for.

The Conversation: "We do everything couples do, but we're not 'official.' What is this?" "He says he's not ready for a relationship but doesn't want me dating anyone else."

Anecdote: Kelsey created a flowchart titled "What Even Are We?" and used it during wine night with her friends to determine whether to DTR (define the relationship) or ditch.

Fun Fact: The term "situationship" was added to the Merriam-Webster dictionary in 2023. That's how real the struggle is.

9. Personal Growth and Compatibility

Why Women Talk About It: Being in sync matters; a partner's growth mindset (or lack thereof) can make or break the future.

The Conversation: "He's great, but he has zero ambition. I don't know if we're growing in the same direction." "He wants to move to Bali and start a goat farm. I just got promoted."

Anecdote: When Allie realized she had read six books on emotional intelligence and her boyfriend still thought "self-help" was a scam, she decided it was time to evolve... solo.

Fun Fact: According to relationship research, couples who grow together tend to stay together. Shared values and mutual goals are better predictors of long-term happiness than shared hobbies.

10. The "He Did WHAT?" Storytime

Why Women Talk About It: Sometimes, you must tell someone your date brought his mom to dinner.

The Conversation: "So I went to his place, and four swords were on the wall. FOUR." "He said he was a 'healer' and tried to bless my aura on the first date."

Anecdote: Lexi once went on a date where the guy ordered for her, corrected her pronunciation of "bruschetta," and asked if she'd "ever considered being less independent." Her group chat response: "I just survived a TED Talk on mansplaining."

Fun Fact: Storytelling is bonding. Sharing ridiculous experiences isn't just entertaining; it strengthens group cohesion and helps people process emotional events.

Our Final Take:

Women talk about men not just to gossip or complain but to connect, decode, laugh, vent, analyze, and sometimes heal. These conversations are rarely about *him* –about *her* needs, growth, joy, doubts, and humor. When women talk about men, they also talk about themselves, each other, and the ever-evolving dance of human connection.

And sometimes, they laugh over that guy with the four swords on his wall as they should.

CHAPTER 14

The New Friendship Frontier

I n many cultures, the whispered secrets and cautious glances exchanged between men and women have long signified an unspoken boundary: friendships across genders were seen as taboo, suspect, or even impossible. Consider Emma and Jack, two coworkers who often found themselves at the same tea station, engrossed in conversations that made the dull hum of office life momentarily disappear. Their discussions ranged from shared interests in books to their love for hiking, each encounter leaving them both re-energized for the workday. Yet, whispers followed them; rumors fueled by colleagues still tethered to archaic views that questioned the legitimacy of their bond. Emma and Jack's encounters were about camaraderie and connection, not romance. But facing a world where societal norms historically painted their kinship with suspicion, they realized their friendship was pioneering new frontiers.

Despite the evolution of gender roles, echoes of past constraints still shape perceptions today. As contemporary societies strive to break traditional molds, redefining these cross-gender friendships becomes essential. This chapter delves into the intricate tapestry of cultural and historical norms that once constrained male-female bonds, examining how they've shaped modern expectations and continue challenging genuine connections. By exploring this transformation, we move towards understanding how friendships evolve amid dynamic social narratives and shifting perceptions.

From Taboo to Truth: Cultural and Historical Norms

Throughout history, male-female friendships have often existed under the shadow of societal norms that defined them in relatively rigid terms. Traditionally, interactions between men and women have been primarily governed by cultural and religious dictates, which, often viewed such relationships with suspicion or relegated them to specific roles. For much of history, the line dividing genders was distinctly drawn by societal rules frequently interpreted through the lens of morality and propriety.

In many cultures, male-female friendships were viewed cautiously, as they were assumed to carry an inherent potential for romantic entanglement. This perception can be traced to societal beliefs entrenched by patriarchal systems, which tend to emphasize control over female sexuality and interaction. For example, during the Victorian era in England, the idea of a platonic relationship was scarcely entertained outside familial connections. Social engagements often occurred in strictly controlled environments to ensure conformity to societal expectations, limiting genuine friendships between men and women.

Cultural differences across the globe highlight the varying degrees of acceptance and resistance to friendships between men and women. In certain Western cultures, efforts to loosen the reins date back to the early 20th century when women gained more autonomy, which began to blur the lines that had traditionally kept the sexes apart. In contrast, highly collectivist societies often prioritized family and communal needs over individual relationships, sometimes enforcing more rigid gender boundaries. In places like Japan and parts of Africa, traditional norms historically dictated that interactions between men and women be limited, especially outside wedlock. These cultural constructs dictated the nature of relationships and set boundaries for interaction, making cross-gender friendships a rare phenomenon.

Male-female friendships were influenced by the societal expectations and roles prescribed to each gender. Society often expected women to be more nurturing and men more independent, setting parameters within which friendships could develop. Feminism in the 1960s and 70s sparked a gradual transformation as women began challenging societal norms and demanding equal rights, including the right to engage in mixed-gender social interactions, freely engage in mixed-gender social interactions, and engage in mixed-gender social interactions. This period marked a cultural shift, allowing friendships to evolve as women entered the workforce more significantly, creating more chances for women and men to form non-romantic relationships in professional settings.

Analyzing these historical norms shows how they shaped the behaviors and expectations in male-female friendships. For instance, Western societies in the 19th century might permit social gatherings but frowned upon private meetings between unmarried men and women. The social condemnation of such friendships was tied closely to the concept of female virtue and male honor, both seen as qualities easily compromised outside traditional interaction settings, such as familial or marital relationships.

The idea that male-female relationships primarily serve as a prelude to something romantic or sexual persisted until much later in modern history. Following World War II, the increased mingling of genders through educational and work opportunities helped evolve perceptions of such relationships. For example, cross-gender friendships became more common on college campuses in the United States, where evolving social norms began accepting the idea of a platonic relationship between the sexes as academically and socially beneficial.

Real-life accounts provide deeper insights into how these friendships have adapted or resisted traditional confines. Anecdotes from the women's rights movement offer examples of women who formed close relationships with male allies based on shared political objectives rather than traditional romantic inclinations. Similarly, workplaces became another setting where friendships could develop, as shared professional challenges created bonds akin to those found in same-gender friendships.

While traditional norms have deeply influenced male-female interactions, shifts towards more open, platonic friendships emerged as part of broader cultural developments. This included the introduction of more diverse gender roles and the questioning of strictly binary views of gender, which cleared a path for friendship dynamics to change. The recognition of friendships featuring a balance of emotional support and understanding; characteristics historically attributed to 'feminine,' or 'masculine' constructs became more widely acceptable.

The evolution of friendship norms has direct implications for contemporary interactions. At their core, friendships between men and women increasingly mirror same-gender friendships, with mutual support and shared interests at the forefront. This shift suggests a paradigm change: rather than relationships being confined by societal dictates, individuals reshape them based on personal compatibilities and reciprocal fulfilment.

As society continues evolving, these shifts highlight the intrinsic value friendships bring beyond conventional relationship boundaries. However, historical norms still subtly influence modern perceptions, as certain stereotypes persist regarding potential romantic involvement between men and women friends. These norms often stem from ingrained cultural beliefs or media representations that seldom stray far from the traditional view of gender relationships being romantic.

The historical backdrop of male-female friendships continues to impact current perceptions. From an era dominated by strict social barriers and cultural stigmas, friendships today can navigate a more accepting landscape, yet the echoes of traditional beliefs remain. As we move forward, understanding the influence of religion, patriarchy, and popular culture on friendships can further open discussions on how these relationships sustain their value amidst evolving societal narratives.

Influence of Religion, Patriarchy, and Pop Culture

In examining the historical backdrop that has shaped contemporary perceptions of male-female friendships, the previous section explored cultural and historical norms to set the stage. This foundation allows us to delve into how religion, patriarchal structures, and popular culture have further framed these interactions.

Religion has long been a defining force, influencing societal norms and individual behaviors. Religious doctrines often delineate strict gender roles, creating boundaries that shape expectations between men and women. For instance, many interpretations of religious texts emphasize roles that keep men and women apart, either by stressing separate familial duties or by promoting the idea of complementarity, which can discourage platonic friendships. For example, traditional Christian teachings frequently promote male leadership within the family, indirectly shaping public behavior by discouraging too intimate a connection between unmarried men and women outside marriage. Similarly,

Islamic traditions may promote observing gender segregation in social settings, impacting how friendships develop. While meaningful to believers, such doctrines have historically tethered male-female interactions to romantic or familial arenas rather than allowing genuine platonic relationships to flourish.

Patriarchy intertwines deeply with religious influences to maintain and control gender relations. This social structure perpetuates a hierarchy where male dominance assumes a central role, often limiting the scope of friendships. Patriarchal systems embed a notion that interactions between men and women inevitably lead to romantic relations, clearly evidenced by societal expectations. Careers dominated by one gender frequently discourage close personal relationships with colleagues of the opposite gender, assuming suspicion towards platonic intentions likely influenced by ingrained patriarchal biases. Literature supports this, recalling laws or customs where men possess authority that diminishes women to merely romantic roles, leaving little room for friendship. This societal backdrop has pushed the narrative that male-female friendships ought to contain an element of romantic potential, contrasting with the natural development of meaningful, non-romantic relationships.

Popular culture is influential in weaving these threads into the modern psyche, presenting vivid portrayals of male-female friendships otherwise missing in our reality. Through media, films, and literature, the portrayal of these interactions largely echoes historical restraints while reinforcing stereotypes. Sitcoms provide a precise case study, often embedding romantic tension into friendships for dramatic effect. Think of Ross and Rachel, Harry, and Sally; their platonic connections immediately viewed under the lens of "When will they?" rather than, "Will they ever?" We succumb to these stories, perpetuating societal standards that all male-female friendships are potential romances barely concealed under the guise of friendship. The constant portrayal of "friends to lovers" tropes leads people to believe that cross-gender friendships cannot remain just friendships, skewing real-world interactions.

Examining religious tenets, patriarchal hierarchies, and portrayals in popular culture reveals a tapestry of influence that restricts the concept of male-female friendship to romantic or limited exchanges. These influences intersect, echoing each other's narratives and having significant real-life implications. Culturally imposed barriers ensure individuals often misinterpret genuine platonic gestures as a potential romantic interest, affecting how men and women perceive their friendships. This impels people toward a cautious line of engagement, keeping their guard up, reducing these friendships to merely functional or obligated roles, like work colleagues or family relations. This hesitance reflects shared anxieties derived from historical narratives and media depictions, showcasing how ingrained these beliefs are.

Recognizing the impacts of religious imperatives, patriarchal norms, and popular storytelling offers a necessary dialogue towards evolving these perceptions. Understanding the root causes allows society to rethink the framing of gender interactions. The historic alliance between these forces cannot be untwined overnight, yet awareness is crucial to encouraging the natural development of these friendships, free from obligatory romantic undertones.

The narrative appears to be shifting. Emerging societal perspectives embrace gender-inclusive friendships. Young generations, more attuned to equality, challenge patriarchal norms and religious mandates that keep dividing genders. New portrayals in the media start reflecting friendships without the obligatory romantic arc, helping unravel stereotypes one plot at a time. The ground begins to soften, providing a bed for male-female friendships to sprout in their own right. This creates a natural transition to the next part of the discussion: the slow, steady move towards societal acceptance of presuming friendship over romance. Male-female friendships can exist as pure connections. As we examine how these fresh perspectives forge new paths, it becomes evident that fostering openness in defining these relationships will be essential. Drawing from the lessons of history and storytelling informs us and empowers us to reshape these old norms into something inclusive and forward-looking. The upcoming section explores this paradigm shift, analyzing how, gradually, society is learning to view these friendships without the implicit assumption of romantic undertones, thereby mislabeling them.

Shift Toward Gender-Inclusive Friendships and Society's Mislabeling

Religion and patriarchy have historically shaped the way we perceive male-female friendships. Popular culture continues enforcing traditional views, reinforcing that certain boundaries are inherent and unavoidable. The idea that "men and women can't just be friends" seems hardwired into society's collective mind, a product of a longstanding narrative crafted by culture, religion, and media. From movies that depict male-female friendships inevitably turning romantic to TV shows that present such relationships with an undercurrent of sexual tension, myths and stereotypes saturate our screens and shape societal norms. These narratives often portray friendships as steppingstones or preludes to romantic entanglements.

Movies like "When Harry Met Sally" and series such as "Friends" and "How I Met Your Mother" have perpetuated this myth by suggesting friendship inevitably leads to romance. Though entertaining, they cement problematic stereotypes that friendships must culminate into something more intimate. These portrayals seep into society, fostering the expectation that genuine friendship devoid of romantic interest is impossible. This leaves little room for platonic bonds and obscures the potential of such friendships, creating barriers to forming authentic connections.

Further, media plays a crucial role in locking people into traditional gender roles, where men need to be providers and women nurturers. These roles subtly influence our interactions and relationships. By suggesting that cross-gender friendships are unnatural, we limit opportunities for emotional growth and understanding. The stereotype that men and women cannot simply be friends upends the potential for relationships where traditional gender expectations do not overshadow individual identities. Instead, these friendships can be spaces where people explore multifaceted human connections.

For example, "Harry Potter" presents a different male-female dynamic in Harry and Hermione's relationship. Their friendship remains steadfastly platonic and deeply supportive throughout the series. Such depictions challenge the notion that sexual tension must always be an underlying theme, demonstrating that deep platonic connections are both possible and enriching. However, these narratives remain exceptional rather than the norm. Despite some progress in media representations, there is still a considerable bias towards portraying these friendships as short-lived or bound to evolve into something else.

Take the myth that men are overtly sexual, and women are emotional. Such stereotypes complicate friendships, where actions or words are misread due to constructed gender roles. Genuine friendship relies on communication free from assumptions about intent or character based on gender. But when people internalize these gendered stereotypes, interpreting platonic gestures becomes ensnared by the need to categorize actions as indicative of romantic interest.

Media perpetuates these stereotypes and influences individual perceptions and behaviors in society. Consequently, people may mimic what they see. This creates a cycle where misunderstandings about friendships based on gender persist, and media content continues to be made that reflects these misconceptions. These portrayals stop authentic friendships from forming by using societal norms as a filter through which interactions are interpreted.

By entrenching the idea that romantic intentions must exist, society creates an environment where cross-gender friendships are scrutinized rather than celebrated. This scrutiny stifles the opportunity to experience diverse relationships that expand personal growth and empathy. When we persistently define friendships along romantic lines, we fail to appreciate them in their own right. This lack of appreciation inhibits the relationships' ability to nurture different perspectives and understanding among genders; an aspect vital in today's world, where knowledge and empathy are paramount.

Challenging these stereotypes requires recognizing the power of platonic friendships as standalone relationships that can exist independently of romantic interest. Discussions around male-female friendships need reframing to emphasize their potential as platforms for mutual support and empathy. In literature and media, we need more nuanced portrayals that recognize these relationships' complexity without forcing them into predefined roles dictated by societal myths about gender.

Such reframing extend to how friendships can redefine misconceptions about emotional sharing. Cross-gender friendships provide a canvas for diverse emotional expressions, breaking free from roles that declare men as stoic and women as emotional. These dynamics allow for friendship interactions characterized by equality and mutual respect, offering alternative models of emotional engagement which step beyond gender biases.

In the following discussion, it's essential to consider how evolving communication methods, such as social media and digital platforms like FaceTime and texting, interact with these narratives. On one hand, such technologies continue to create and disseminate stereotypes rapidly. Yet, they also offer new opportunities for shaping interactions in a world increasingly interconnected by screens and keyboards. Moreover, they redefine how we maintain and perceive relationships, stepping away from traditional methods driven by proximity, with the potential to forge new avenues for male-female friendships rooted in genuine, authentic connection rather than cultural legend.

Recognizing these factors can lead to understanding how to actively dismantle myths by portraying male-female friendships as multifaceted relationships. These friendships should be based on a blend of similarities and differences, shedding traditional gender expectations. If the media and societal narratives reflect more of these realities, they help forge pathways toward redefining male-female friendships within a modern, inclusive context. By breaking free from stereotypes, these friendships can evolve unencumbered by expectations and grow into reciprocal and supportive connections. As we move further into this new age of connectivity, recognizing platonic friendships' value is crucial in shaping a more understanding and empathically connected society.

Stereotypes, Myths, and Media Expectations

In the journey towards gender-inclusive friendships, society continuously grapples with the decades-old stereotype that "men and women can't just be friends." This myth persists due in large part to the media's portrayal of cross-gender interactions. Media representations often underpin these stereotypes by placing friendships between men and women into narrow boxes, rarely acknowledging the possibility of platonic relationships. This portrayal fuels societal expectations, crafting a narrative that discourages platonic intimacy between genders.

Media often reinforces these myths through repetitive storytelling that underscores romantic tension as an inevitable outcome of close relationships between men and women. The narrative generally unfolds in a way that suggests friendship is merely a precursor to romance, sidelining the genuine potential of platonic bonds. These portrayals have seeped into cultural consciousness so much that they often influence how individuals perceive and engage in friendships with the opposite gender.

For instance, in television programming and movies, plotlines frequently revolve around friends who eventually realize their "true" romantic feelings for one another, negating the viability of sustaining platonic friendships. This framework leaves a faint footprint on societal perception, implying that any deep connection between men and women must culminate in romantic engagement. Despite evolving gender roles in society, wherein women are increasingly recognized for their competencies and contributions, the media lags in reflecting these shifts, frequently portraying women in traditional or recreational roles rather than professional equals to their male counterparts.

In children's television and other media, male representation often eclipses females, establishing early on a skewed perspective of gender roles. Boys and girls internalize these representations, which can translate into distorted and dated perceptions about friendship dynamics as they mature. Consequently, cross-gender friendships remain overshadowed by stereotypical portrayals, leading to skepticism and misconceptions about their plausibility.

Beyond television, advertising perpetuates gender stereotypes by depicting men in authoritative, professional roles and women in more stereotypical feminine contexts, which reinforces outdated notions about gender capabilities and relationships. Advertising and media portrayals often act in concert, further entrenching notions that intimacy and vulnerability in cross-gender interactions inherently lead to romantic feelings. Resulting perceptions can manifest as barriers to forming meaningful friendships, where both parties might hesitate to connect deeply on a platonic level.

Social media and contemporary communication methods provide a counterbalance to these pervasive stereotypes. Digital platforms and communication tools like texting and FaceTime allow people to engage without physical presence, reducing romantic tensions emphasized in face-to-face interactions. These methods provide an evolving narrative on how individuals from different genders can maintain robust, platonic bonds. They normalize conversations that don't rely on physical cues often interpreted in traditional media as signals of romantic interest.

Studies have shown that friendships are essential in promoting emotional balance and expanding empathy. The idea is that understanding different perspectives—regardless of gender—leads to more harmonious relationships across the board. Cross-gender friendships create gender-neutral spaces rich in learning and mutual respect when allowed to flourish without romantic overtones.

This transformation is crucial. Modern communication tools offer opportunities to redefine these friendships as face-to-face dynamics shift. They allow individuals to set comfortable boundaries, devoid of the outdated limitations media typically assigns to cross-gender interactions. Moreover, digital interactions foster emotional bonds that might otherwise succumb to geographical distance or societal expectations about friendship roles.

While media narratives continue to evolve, they must catch up with the real-world progress privileging equality and mutual respect over stereotypes. Bridging the gap between expectation and reality requires intentional representation, emphasizing friendship as an entity independent of romantic entanglement. The depiction of cross-gender friendships must evolve from a mere subplot in romantic storylines to a standalone narrative celebrating the multifaceted potential of these relationships.

Increasing such representations in media normalizes them, paving the way for societal perceptions to shift. It transforms societal expectations, breaking down myths that have long dictated how individuals from different genders interact. Moving towards acknowledging the deep and varied nature of friendships challenges stereotypes, building new norms that allow for honest, transparent cross-gender interactions.

As we understand the importance of friendship for emotional health, modern communication tools will play a vital role. They establish channels for straightforward interactions, allowing friendships to develop organically. These tools help create a culture where boundaries are understood and respected, aligning with modern values prioritizing gender equality and collaborative understanding.

Thus, the potential for friendships between genders to evolve into supportive, enriching relationships rests on shattering stereotypes and embracing communication methods that facilitate genuine connections. The emphasis on connection and understanding enriches personal and collective experiences, shaping a future where friendships flourish without being shadowed by unfounded myths. Modern communication tools bridge tangible gaps and catalyst a deeper exploration of friendships' potential in creating balanced lives filled with empathy and equal opportunity.

Importance in Modern Times and Digital Connections

In the previous section, we dismantled myths placing male-female friendships under societal scrutiny. Historically, narratives have unfairly labelled these relationships as precursors to romance, trivializing their profound impact. Today, these friendships stand out for their significance in emotional stability, empathy improvement, and forming gender-neutral spaces, especially as technology reshapes how we connect and communicate.

Male-female friendships are crucial in today's world, offering unique emotional benefits that stem from diverse perspectives. These exchanges encourage empathy and mutual support, often recognizing and bridging emotional gaps that might exist in same-gender friendships. Through understanding different experiences, individuals develop a more nuanced view of the world, contributing to personal growth and emotional balance.

Communication technologies have become essential in evolving these friendships. Platforms like texting, memes, and

FaceTime act as modern bridges, connecting individuals across physical and emotional distances. Consider the simplicity and convenience of sending a meme. It doesn't just entertain; it conveys personality and emotion, fostering a sense of shared culture and humor. Texting enables immediate support or sharing experiences, reflecting a shift from traditional communication barriers.

Technology facilitates a nurturing space where casual conversations can flourish into significant relationships. This evolution is visible as individuals utilize these platforms to transcend physical presence limitations. Modern tools allow real-time communication and flexibility in interaction, maintaining bonds even when geography is a barrier. Individuals find that the ability to connect frequently contributes to sustained and deepened interactions.

Male-female friendships in this digital age have reshaped traditional communication, allowing for rich interactions that would have been cumbersome or impossible before. The immediacy of digital tools offers a channel for maintaining intimacy and responsiveness, which texts and video calls readily provide. For instance, video calls enhance the exchange of social cues, unlike text-based communication, which sometimes lacks emotional depth. This enriched communication is critical, especially when exploring more profound personal matters.

Concerning boundaries, technology must enable interactions without overstepping personal limits. These tools must support healthy boundaries that sustain the autonomy of both individuals. Digital platforms place communication control in the users' hands, determining when and how to engage, thus preventing overwhelming or boundary violations. This autonomy ensures that interactions remain healthy and consented to, laying a robust foundation for honest connections.

Gender dynamics within these friendships foster mutual understanding, breaking down conventional perceptions. With platforms facilitating open dialogue, individuals can transcend gender norms, gaining insight into experiences distinct from their own. This understanding helps construct gender-neutral spaces where both men and women feel equally empowered to express themselves, challenging and deconstructing traditional gender roles.

These friendships create platforms that emphasize support and understanding in a world where gender roles can restrict interactions. By engaging with diverse communication that technology allows, individuals realize how gender roles are not barriers but components of broader societal structures they can collaboratively navigate and influence. This dynamic contributes to healthy interactions founded on shared respect and equality.

While the digital aspect of these friendships is transformative, it's essential to distinguish between virtual and physical presence. The latter holds an indisputable value that technology cannot replicate. However, with virtual tools, the frequency and uniqueness of interactions can compensate for physical absence. They do not replace face-to-face encounters but enhance friendships' depth and breadth by filling gaps caused by time and distance constraints.

Frequent engagements over digital platforms enhance emotional closeness, allowing individuals to share immediate moments, sentiments, and experiences in ways that traditional forms couldn't accommodate. These interactions often lead to elevated understanding and support, thus strengthening relational bonds. The virtual realm provides a new layer, allowing intentional sharing, from simple status updates to significant personal milestones.

Daily interactions sometimes need comprehensive efforts to remind individuals of their presence in each other's lives. The digital world assists in maintaining regular connections, ensuring continuity in relationships, and minimizing the effects of physical separation, such as loneliness or isolation. This regularity promotes a shared life experience vital for emotional well-being and the sustained growth of any friendship.

In detailing these relationships, an evolving communication landscape emerges. These digital friendships help neutralize gender constructs, foster mutual understanding, and offer platforms for bridging emotional and physical gaps. The tales we share, our digital spaces, and the emotional support we exchange reflect a transformed friendship landscape where everyone constructs inclusive, empowering connections.

Technology offers not a replacement but an enhancement of our social realities. Navigating this new terrain allows male-female friendships to thrive, characterized by respectful boundaries, growing empathy, and genuine connection. As we embrace the digital spectrum, the virtual becomes a conduit, enriching friendships and aligning with their natural evolution toward emotional collaboration and enlightenment.

Concluding Thoughts

As we navigate the evolving landscape of male-female friendships in a changing world, it's clear that historical norms and stereotypes have long skewed how these relationships are perceived. However, as society progresses, so does our understanding that these friendships can be valuable, enriching connections beyond traditional boundaries. The steady shift towards gender-inclusive friendships fueled by technology and modern communication methods redefines interactions between men and women. This paradigm change highlights the importance of viewing male-female friendships not as preludes to romance but as multifaceted bonds that offer empathy, support, and mutual growth. By embracing this new perspective, we pave the way for more genuine connections that defy outdated societal expectations. As we move forward, recognizing the intrinsic value of these friendships can contribute to more inclusive and empathetic interpersonal dynamics, enhancing the fabric of a diverse and interconnected society.

CHAPTER 15

Building the Bond

Sarah and Tom had been friends since college, sharing hobbies and stories without a hint of romantic tension. Their friendship was easygoing, flourishing over shared study sessions and weekend hiking trips. Yet, occasional whispers from friends insisted that a man and woman couldn't remain just friends, nudging them to consider the "inevitable" romantic spark. To Sarah and Tom, this notion seemed laughable, as their bond was grounded in mutual respect and clear boundaries, not clouded by unspoken desires.

Despite societal pressures, they maintained a seamless dynamic, even as they navigated career changes and geographic moves. Their connection thrived on honesty—check-ins about their comfort levels and intentions were routine. They understood each other's communication style, which helped them sidestep potential pitfalls that could blur lines into something unintended. Their balance was delicate, yet it showcased how genuine male-female friendships could flourish when approached with care. This chapter will explore how these platonic relationships begin and flourish while emphasizing the importance of setting boundaries and maintaining clear communication to preserve their unique nature.

Breaking the Ice without Mixed Signals

Navigating the early stages of platonic male-female friendships requires a nuanced understanding of how these relationships often begin and how to maintain their unique dynamics. Frequently, such friendships are sparked through shared interests, activities, or environments, such as workplaces, hobby groups, or mutual social circles. Given the socio-cultural expectations surrounding relationships between men and women, it's crucial to approach these budding friendships with clarity and purpose.

When you first enter a potential platonic friendship, setting mutual expectations is key to fostering understanding and preventing misinterpretation. Instead of allowing assumptions to shape the trajectory of your relationship, engage in candid conversations about your intentions. This proactive approach signals respect for one another's perspectives and creates a foundational level of trust. For instance, if you meet someone through a hobby such as running, you might frame your shared interest as the focal point of your interactions, emphasizing the enjoyment of the activity rather than allowing the relationship to evolve into another form unintentionally.

The role of clear communication cannot be overstated, especially in the beginning. Platonic friendships thrive on transparency. Recognizing that non-verbal cues can sometimes convey more than words, pay close attention to the body language you exhibit and perceive from your friend. Subtle gestures like maintaining eye contact, an open posture, and respectful physical distance signal engagement and consideration, promoting a comfortable atmosphere that echoes mutual respect. Misreading these cues can inadvertently lead to misunderstandings, underscoring the need for conscious awareness of your and your friend's body language.

Beyond interpreting body language, energy dynamics play a pivotal role in sustaining platonic friendships. "energy" refers to the vibe or emotional atmosphere during interactions. Respecting each other's energy involves honoring your friend's personal boundaries and emotional states, which might evolve throughout the friendship. Empathetic listening and regular check-ins can help you meet each other's expectations and emotional needs. This process is pivotal for nurturing friendships built on independence and support rather than dependence, affirming the voluntary nature of these bonds.

Intentionality further shapes the beginnings of male-female friendships. Take, for instance, a work colleague with whom you've developed a rapport. Transitioning from casual conversations about job responsibilities to more personal topics requires a conscious decision to deepen the relationship without undercutting the platonic framework. It's about allowing the connection to progress naturally while remaining sensitive to mutual boundaries and maintaining open lines of communication to check in on the alignment of intentions.

Empathy and open communication are critical to initial platonic dynamics and gradually prepare the way for emotional safety. People often hesitate to open up immediately, fearing vulnerability might lead to disrespect or overfamiliarity. It's crucial to balance self-disclosure with mutual acceptance, grappling with the paradox of independence and dependence in relationships. By respecting each other's autonomy while offering support, friends can find a satisfying equilibrium where emotional expression feels comfortable and accepted.

Physical manifestations of this stage include casual social outings beyond initial meeting settings, illustrating the transition from a work friendship to a more informal one. Using the example of a colleague, inviting them for coffee after shared work hours emphasizes interest in expanding the relationship, indicating a voluntary shift beyond workplace roles. This shift signals appreciation of each other's company in varied contexts, potentially strengthening the foundational bond.

As this friendship state matures, maintaining spontaneity and embracing minor deviations from formal interactions supports the progression toward a richer connection. Trust becomes a hallmark of the evolving friendship, buoyed by mutual disclosures and the understanding that these exchanges remain respected and reciprocal. This evolution stems from the balance between affection and instrumentality, reinforcing the importance of aligning personal and shared needs within relationships for balanced satisfaction.

Recognizing your friend's strengths and individuality enriches the interactional experience, as validation of each other's unique qualities bolsters emotional connection and shared growth. Hearing a colleague share a joke or personal news highlights that organic expression of self has merged with professional interactions, signifying deepening trust and friendship quality.

Transitions towards more profound vulnerability often coincide with a growing willingness to tackle complex subjects or personal struggles, a testament to the friendship's established sense of emotional safety. To achieve such depth, both parties must remain active listeners, facilitating an environment where honest disclosure is met with empathy and unconditional acceptance.

As you explore these dimensions, let this groundwork introduce you to the subsequent topic. Transition into understanding how further deepening of platonic male-female friendships can occur through fostering emotional safety, leading conversations to encompass more personal issues. Emphasizing emotional availability and mutual support systems sets the stage for engaging with and nurturing friendship and individual authenticity on a profound new level.

Emotional Safety and Vulnerability

In the last section, we considered how shared interests, work, or hobbies often serve as the starting point for new friendships. At this juncture, let's focus on emotional safety and vulnerability. In any friendship, especially between males and females, creating a safe space where both parties feel supported to express their true feelings is crucial. However, it's equally important to ensure that this safety doesn't blur the lines of a platonic relationship. Allowing vulnerability often strengthens bonds, but emotional openness must be balanced by awareness of personal and shared boundaries.

Emotional safety forms the bedrock of any friendship. It means establishing a trust-rich environment where both friends can share personal insights and experiences without fear of judgment or misunderstanding. Mutual respect is at the core: understanding each other's history, emotional availability, and readiness to engage deeply. Notably, openness may inadvertently lead some to misinterpret platonic intimacies as romantic. Thus, it's vital to maintain clear communication channels to prevent potential confusion.

Creating emotional safety demands self-awareness. Be cognizant of why you're opening up and what you expect in return. Importantly, assess whether your friend is emotionally available to support you. This mutual assessment can prevent lopsided emotional exchanges that often lead to complications. For example, imagine John and Sarah, who share a close friendship. John recently experienced a breakup and usually finds solace in Sarah's understanding. While Sarah offers support, she notices her emotional well-being being drained. Sarah must communicate boundaries, ensuring their friendship remains balanced and does not become burdensome for either party.

Maintaining friendship boundaries often starts with open dialogues about emotional expectations and comfort levels. Men and women being friends sometimes tread complex waters; society usually expects platonic ties to evolve romantically. Therefore, having conversations on expectations can clarify the nature of your bond. Addressing emotional boundaries candidly reinforces that even their deepest confessions don't alter the friendship's non-romantic status—a pivotal understanding to prevent tension and misaligned expectations.

Friends navigating this space often advocate for each other's growth and stability. For instance, investing in active listening; one friend attentively processing the other's fears without judgment while providing sound advice can be supportive and reassuring. Additionally, establishing regular check-ins where each asks about the other's well-being smooths potential emotional rough patches before they develop into more significant issues.

Vulnerability does not imply emotional dependency, nor should it become a one-sided release valve for personal struggles. It's a shared experience fostering connection without crossing emotional thresholds. Friends who are honest about their feelings create intimacy rooted in respect rather than possessiveness.

In friendships, assuring each other of the relationship's platonic nature—similar to affirming romantic commitment—can reduce anxiety and prevent misunderstandings. In another context, dedication as a facet of relational commitment emphasized by Stanley et al. parallels the importance of commitment to platonic boundaries in friendships when both parties actively nurture the bond while being dedicated to maintaining its platonic nature.

Friendships thrive on the exercise of personal autonomy within mutually respected boundaries. Ultimately, part of emotional safety includes fostering personal growth by supporting each other's explorative journeys without intruding. Encouraging each other's endeavors is one example of actively enhancing each other's life quality without encroaching upon personal emotional sovereignty.

One approach to maintaining emotional safety is consistent with the idea that fulfilling relationships benefit from affirming communication and affirmational behavior: applicable as much to friendships as romantic relationships. A weekly reflective session where friends exchange appreciation for each other, similar to the "State of the Union" meeting for couples. During these engagements, friends express gratitude, discuss avenues for deepening connections, and address potential boundaries. This approach nurtures emotional safety and solidifies the friendship's non-romantic facet.

Our understanding of emotional safety naturally progresses into recognizing healthy platonic boundaries. Awareness of how we express emotions within our friendships directly informs how we draw these lines. As we transition to the "Healthy Boundaries 101" section, solidifying emotional safety must entail an examination of physical, emotional, and digital boundaries, thereby enhancing mutual respect. We'll explore how these distinctions ensure clarity in intentions and guard against overstepping.

Healthy boundaries in friendships define the limits within which emotional safety flourishes and provide a structured autonomy necessary for personal growth and mutual satisfaction. Discussions about appropriate expressions of platonic affection, the healthy extent of emotional sharing, and ensuring digital interactions respect privacy will form the next critical steps. Building boundaries that accommodate both friends' needs ensures emotional safety and meets personal authenticity without compromising the platonic essence pulling the friendship forward.

In summary, prioritizing emotional safety and vulnerability within friendships demands efforts toward clear communication, setting mutual expectations, and reinforcing non-romantic intentions. These actions build a supportive structure for emotional exchanges to thrive without crossing intimacy borders. As we seamlessly embrace "Healthy Boundaries 101," understanding the balance between emotional safety and boundaries will equip us to maintain connections free of confusion and full of authenticity.

Healthy Boundaries 101

Setting boundaries upfront helps prevent misunderstandings and reinforces mutual respect, fostering friendships where both parties feel secure and valued. By understanding personality and gender nuances, we can enhance the mutual support systems vital to maintaining these friendships.

Men and women often approach friendships differently, though it's important to note these are general observations rather than strict rules. Typically, men may lean towards side-by-side interactions, engaging in shared activities or interests, whereas women often connect through face-to-face communication, emphasizing emotional sharing and verbal interaction. This variance doesn't just stem from gender, personal tendencies, and social conditioning. Acknowledging this can create empathy and understanding, allowing both parties to support each other's friendship needs more effectively.

For instance, imagine a friendship where the male is more activity-oriented, preferring to catch a game together or embark on a shared hobby. Meanwhile, the female friend might be inclined towards heartfelt conversations over coffee. Recognizing and respecting these preferences can deepen their connection. Perhaps they can alternate activities; one day engaged in dynamic activities and another catching up over meals. This approach respects individual preferences and strengthens the friendship by allowing each friend to feel understood and valued. This mutual acknowledgement reinforces personal bonds and merges diverse interests, enriching the friendship dynamic.

Open discussion about these differences also plays a pivotal role. Encouraging straightforward communication prevents assumptions and misunderstandings. It's about bringing authenticity to the table. Rather than guessing, friends can express, "I feel most connected when we talk openly," or "Activities make me feel closer to you." These declarations help mold the friendship into a safe space where both parties can interact comfortably without sacrificing their connection style.

Understanding personality dichotomies, such as introversion versus extroversion, adds another layer to navigating friendships. An introverted individual might value calm, intimate settings, while their extroverted friend thrives in lively environments filled with people. This awareness enables them to create tailored experiences that satisfy both needs. Perhaps they might choose a small gathering one evening and a bustling event the next, balancing tranquility and excitement.

Divergent emotional expressions also require empathy and consideration. Typically, men might express their feelings through actions, favoring subtle shows of camaraderie or gestures of help, while women might navigate feelings more verbally, seeking dialogue for emotional processing. Encouraging open conversation rather than guessing motives or waiting for expressions ensures clarity. This communication might manifest in one friend asking directly, "How can I support you?" or sharing observations like, "I notice when you do this, it makes me feel respected."

When embraced, these approaches subvert potential conflicts arising from unarticulated expectations. They also create a strong foundation wherein platonic bonds can thrive without the pitfalls of miscommunication. Strong friendships hinge on recognizing and bridging these differences with empathy and dialogue.

Furthermore, gender expectations can sometimes bring unspoken pressures to friendships; stereotypes suggesting men shouldn't express vulnerability or women shouldn't show assertiveness. Friends should encourage each other to defy these norms, supporting expressions that feel authentic and liberating for their friends. It might mean helping a friend through emotional vulnerability or appreciating acts of assertiveness without judgment.

Navigating assumptions requires patience and a commitment to directness. Instead of reacting to perceived slights or absences, a better approach involves communication that removes room for misunderstandings. This might include declaring what each friend values most in interactions or choosing to address changes in behavior immediately. Statements like, "I felt there was a shift when..." initiate honest discussions and prevent festering assumptions.

As friendships grow, it's crucial to maintain a continuous dialogue about evolving preferences or boundaries. Friendships thrive on the conscious effort to update each other on changes in comfort levels or interests, adapting to who each individual is becoming. Regular check-ins nurture these relationships and express a willingness to evolve alongside each other, ensuring neither party feels stuck in outdated perceptions.

Having established how these dynamics of friendship styles operate, we now prepare to explore "When Feelings Enter the Chat." Understanding gender-specific friendship dynamics lays the groundwork for navigating emotional shifts. If platonic feelings begin evolving, having practiced open communication and boundary recognition aids in managing these transitions with understanding and sensitivity. Encouraging reflection on how comfort with each other's uniqueness contributes to a more profound emotional growth allows friends to handle these changes thoughtfully.

Conclusively, recognizing, and respecting gender and personality influences within friendships enriches interactions and emotional connections. By navigating differences through active and authentic communication, friends foster supportive, balanced, and enduring relationships. In doing so, they create an environment where friendships can adapt gracefully to changes, deepening trust, and appreciation for each other's company.

Friendship Styles by Gender (and Personality)

Acknowledging and respecting platonic boundaries in friendships is pivotal. Just as boundaries serve as the framework ensuring respect, understanding how men and women connect in friendships is essential to preventing misunderstandings that can strain these relationships. It's interesting how societal norms and gender roles shape how we express and process emotions differently. Men and women often vary significantly in emotional expressions, leading to misinterpretations if not thoughtfully navigated. For instance, while women may express emotions more openly, men might prefer to process feelings internally, influences possibly tied to societal expectations.

Research highlights these gender-related differences in emotional expression from an early age. Girls are often encouraged to display emotions such as empathy and nurturing behaviors and learn a different kind of emotional vocabulary than boys, who might lean towards expressing strength and composure. These ingrained behaviors can impact adulthood friendships, where men might express emotions through actions rather than words, potentially leading to misinterpretations. Understanding these nuances, rooted partly in childhood developmental scripts, helps recognize the genuine intentions behind each other's actions.

In a friendship setting, one might expect inherent ease only to encounter complexities stemming from these differences. Suppose a woman expresses concern or care for her male friend during a challenging time while he interprets it within the confines of needing to maintain emotional independence. Rather than leading to misunderstanding, this situation, with awareness, can open discussions about differing needs in friendship. Such dialogue can fortify the relationship, fostering a more profound connection that respects these emotional differences. Social constructionist theories underscore the importance of context, showing how these interactions don't merely arise within a vacuum but are shaped by more considerable societal expectations.

Open communication is central to fostering understanding across these gender lines. When both parties feel comfortable voicing their perspectives, assumptions give way to clarity. Instead of assuming a friend is uninterested due to a lack of verbal response, a conversation clarifying emotional expression styles can reveal underlying sentiments, strengthening the bond. In many cases, these discussions prevent the accumulation of unspoken grievances, which, if left unaddressed, might cause rifts. This proactive approach to communication nurtures an environment where both parties feel valued and heard.

Understanding these aspects allows both men and women to interact more genuinely without succumbing to gender-based stereotypes. A practical approach involves creating scenarios where partners can practice this transparent communication and align expectations. For example, consider two friends planning a weekend outing. The woman might openly express her excitement through animated discussion, while the man might nod in agreement, quietly preparing for the day. Without understanding each other's expression styles, the woman might feel her enthusiasm isn't reciprocated. By discussing these variances, they can acknowledge the diversity in expression and set expectations that resonate with both styles.

The role of societal norms can't be understated here. While these norms influence behaviors, our friendships' interactions allow us to challenge and redefine them. During adolescence, these expressive styles are shaped by family and cultural narratives. Sometimes, parents unknowingly can steer children towards certain emotional expressions deemed appropriate. Recognizing this dynamic in friendships propels understanding of how peers influence each other's emotional landscapes.

Having established a foundation of understanding, consider the transformative potential friendships hold in bridging these expressions. For instance, leveraging the ability to mirror each other's responses can balance these dynamics. A male friend can consciously practice verbal affirmations, enhancing mutual comprehension, whereas his female friend might traditionally err towards verbalizing thoughts more freely. This practice demands conscious effort but yields a deepened understanding and appreciation for each other's unique communication style, aligning with the social constructionist lens where context and interaction produce behavior.

Navigating these differences thoughtfully paves the way for rich, mutually respected friendships. It's vital to approach these differences with curiosity rather than defensiveness. Assuming mutual goodwill and recognizing these patterns without letting stereotypes constrain us empowers friendships, allowing them to thrive beyond limited gender narratives. This learning extends to observing other friendships, analyzing what works, and integrating those positive traits into our interactions.

With this base of understanding, it feels organic to hint at complexities beyond maintaining a strictly platonic friendship. Emotional nuances can sometimes evolve, inviting feelings that were unintended initially. Recognizing this potential shift presents an opportunity for honest conversations before misinterpretations muddle the bond. By addressing these shifts before they embed into the relationship dynamic, friends can prevent confusion and maintain the core of their friendship. Direct dialogue about any emerging feelings fortifies the relationship against unforeseen turbulence.

Engaging in these conversations preemptively allows friendships to adapt, maintaining honesty and respect at the relationship's heart. It's less about drawing hard lines and more about recognizing when emotions might cross from platonic to romantic. Willingness to have these conversations sets the stage for maintaining trust and understanding, even as feelings evolve. By broaching potential shifts with openness, friendships continue to flourish, equipped to handle these transitions without losing their essence.

As friendships deepen, understanding these intricate emotional weaving aids in creating relationships that thrive on empathy, communication, and trust. Embarking on these explorations of connection strengthens individual friendships and reshapes how we consider gender and emotional expressions. Consider these reflections an invitation to delve into the dynamic evolution of friendships, enriching them with authenticity and mutual respect, ready to embrace the complexities of when feelings might enter the chat.

When Feelings Enter the Chat

In conversations about emotional expression between men and women, navigating romantic feelings in platonic friendships offers unique challenges and opportunities for growth. When one person starts catching feelings, this delicate scenario requires thoughtfully addressing both parties' emotions. Openness and communication become paramount to ensure these feelings are managed constructively, preserving the friendship and respecting each other's emotional landscape.

Imagine this: you're in a friendship where everything feels effortless and genuine, and then suddenly, one side feels the shift; an unspoken language develops, and emotions evolve. You find yourself wondering whether to keep pretending nothing's changed or whether to address the new stirrings openly. For many, it is the moment when feelings enter the chat, and the uncharted territory of discussing these emotions begins. Caught in a whirlwind of new feelings, gathering your thoughts is vital.

"Talking" serves as the first critical step. This conversation needs to be grounded in honesty and empathy. Expressing romantic interest should start with affirming the existing friendship's value and setting a stage of mutual respect. This act of transparency allows both parties to make informed decisions. It also involves taking a moment to sort through your emotions privately before confronting your friend.

Many fear losing the friendship upon revealing deeper feelings, which is a legitimate concern. However, silence can breed assumptions and misunderstandings and strain the relationship. A carefully phrased conversation lets you articulate your thoughts without putting undue pressure on the other person. Acknowledge the potential awkwardness yet emphasize the importance of honesty for a continued genuine connection.

Consider a scenario where a friend, Alex, has developed feelings for Jamie. Alex values their friendship and doesn't want to harm it by confessing prematurely or indirectly. In a calm setting, Alex might say, "I've appreciated our friendship, and it means a lot to me. I've noticed my feelings changing, and I wanted to share this with you because I think we must be honest with each other, regardless of the outcome." Alex's approach shows respect for Jamie's feelings and the friendship, creating an open arena for dialogue.

Open communication exemplifies maturity and respect even in the face of discomfort. This recognition of vulnerability embodies self-awareness. Should both parties reciprocate these feelings, transitioning from friends to a romantic relationship is complicated. It requires nurturing the pre-existing friendship while embracing new dynamics. This gradual evolution includes fostering deeper emotional connections through meaningful exchanges and shared experiences. Ensuring mutual understanding of aspirations further strengthens this transition, creating a solid foundation for romance.

However, if the feelings aren't mutual, the challenge shifts to preserving the friendship's integrity. It's pivotal to manage emotional responses and acknowledge the other's feelings without taking them personally. Reassure each other of the friendship's continuing value while respecting the need for some space if necessary. Many find consulting external, trusted voices helpful in navigating these complexities, avoiding confusion, and fostering clarity.

Take "Mackenzie" as an example, who confessed feelings to a friend, Alex, who did not feel the same way. They both agreed to step back, allowing Mackenzie time to process the emotions. They stayed in touch through regular but not overwhelming communication, reestablishing a baseline of platonic interactions. Over time, the friendship rebounded with a renewed understanding and respect for each other's boundaries.

Moreover, these conversations can encourage personal growth by refining emotional intelligence and understanding the boundaries between friendship and romance. Openly discussing these feelings also lays the groundwork for evolving dynamics without fostering any resentment. When handled with care, honesty, and transparency, these conversations disclose personal truths that can catalyze deep personal insight.

Ultimately, these challenges revolve around balanced conversations, empathy, and a willingness to embrace potential outcomes positively. Both sides must navigate this transition sensitively, fostering mutual respect and understanding. Emphasizing personal reflection and self-awareness prepares individuals to handle these emotions responsibly, ensuring long-lasting ties that strengthen the friendship, regardless of its current form.

Seizing new romantic possibilities or reaffirming a cherished friendship becomes equally rewarding when respect and communication guide us. Through careful and empathetic dialogue, friends can find strength in vulnerability, ensuring that these pivotal moments are a path to deeper human connections and self-discovery.

Final Thoughts

In exploring the intricacies of starting, deepening, and setting boundaries in platonic male-female friendships, we've delved into the significance of clear communication and mutual understanding. These friendships possess unique dynamics that demand an awareness of personal and social expectations. Engaging in candid dialogues and respecting each other's energy and boundaries can cultivate authentic connections built on trust and independence. As these relationships mature, emotional safety becomes paramount, inviting more profound vulnerability while maintaining the integrity of the platonic nature. Recognizing and respecting these elements lays the groundwork for richer interactions that nurture friendship and individual authenticity. Now equipped with these insights, we are better prepared to navigate the complexities of platonic friendships, ensuring they thrive and enhance our social landscapes.

CHAPTER 16

Future-Proofing the Friendship

Jonathan and Alex had been inseparable since college, sharing everything from late-night debates over pizza to dreams of future ventures. But when Jonathan landed his dream job on the opposite coast, excitement was tinged with a creeping concern about what this distance might mean for their friendship. Initially, there were video calls over breakfast and lengthy text exchanges about their daily lives. However, as time passed and responsibilities grew, those once-frequent conversations dwindled. The miles separating them became more than physical; they signified an emotional gap neither anticipated.

Maintaining friendships can become a precarious balancing act in the ever-changing landscape of adult life. New jobs, relationships, and relocations often push us in directions we hadn't imagined, testing even the most steadfast bonds. As Jonathan and Alex found themselves navigating this new reality, they faced a common dilemma many of us understand: how do you preserve the essence of a friendship amidst life's relentless changes? This chapter delves into strategies for future-proofing friendships, ensuring they remain strong, supportive, and drama-free even as the world evolves.

Friendship in Motion: Adapting to Life Changes

Life changes have a way of rewriting the rules we once knew. New jobs can overhaul our routines, new relationships introduce different priorities, relocations redefine our environments, and parenthood transforms our daily existence.

Each of these changes can alter how friendships function. For many adults, friendships represent steadfastness in a life where everything else evolves perpetually. However, these changes can challenge even the strongest bonds and threaten the sense of connection we cherish.

Picture Jonathan and Alex, friends since their days as college roommates. When Jonathan accepted a dream job on the opposite coast, excitement, and a creeping concern for their friendship's future bubbled. They had shared countless evenings debating life over late-night pizza, but now an entire country lay between them. The initial enthusiasm for Jonathan's new job brought frequent communication; days often started with video calls over breakfast or long texts recounting their lives. Yet, as Jonathan settled into his role and Alex juggled his growing responsibilities at home, the calls gradually became less frequent. Miles of physical distance expanded into an emotional one.

Despite this challenge, both knew that their bond was worth maintaining. They recognized how essential it was to keep their friendship a priority intentionally. Weekly calls restarted as a non-negotiable ritual, marked on respective calendars like any other important commitment. They tried to visit each other in person multiple times a year, discovering that shared experiences helped bridge the gap formed by absence.

Not every story mirrors such a clear path back to connection. Consider the experience of Rachel and Sam, who were inseparable during their single years. When Rachel met someone special, their evenings of spontaneous adventures gave way to planned weekends with her partner. Sam initially felt on the outside looking in. However, instead of allowing feelings of neglect to fester, they addressed the shift openly. They acknowledged the change and adjusted their expectations. Rachel reinforced the message that their friendship remained crucial by involving Sam in her partner's world and maintaining those one-on-one times together.

Major life transitions highlight that friendships can drift if left unattended, but conscious effort can successfully counterbalance such drift. It's about recognizing that these bonds require active participation. This brings us to the underpinning strategy: intentional communication. This means not allowing the flurry of short messages or social media interactions to replace deeper connections. It's not just about talking often but talking meaningfully. Discussing these significant life changes candidly, acknowledging the shifting dynamics, and expressing appreciation for one another's presence. However, it manifests and anchors the relationship.

Flexibility is another key. Each change demands its unique renegotiation of boundaries and priorities. When Katya's career took her from freelancing at home to an executive role in a bustling city office, she found little time for weekday get-togethers with old friends. Rather than drift apart, she and her group established monthly book clubs, incorporating a shared passion. It allowed them to maintain ties within the constraints of Katya's new schedule and find new common ground.

Embracing technology offers another practical tool for navigating life's shifts. Beyond calls and text messages, platforms that allow shared activities; think virtual game nights, collaborative playlists, or watching shows together via apps; mimic physical presence and maintain the bond. Creative ways of connecting with loved ones can be surprisingly simple yet effective in feeling together, even apart.

It's vital to acknowledge that as friendships evolve, so must our perceptions of closeness. Life phases can dictate the frequency and nature of our interactions, but they don't define the depth of our bonds. A friendship matured through change can develop resilience; it understands the ebb and flow of distance and connection. Who says physical presence is the only indicator of commitment?

Transitioning to parenting is a vivid example. Sarah found her world to shift into a whirlwind of new routines, initially leaving her friendships feeling like a distant memory. Friends without children had sympathy but struggled with the abrupt transformation of their weekly happy hours into baby-friendly brunches. Sarah uncovered the support she needed by reaching out and incorporating friends into her new world and being transparent about her capacity and desire for involvement. Those friends who understood visited without expectation, providing camaraderie at hours that suited the erratic early-parent schedule.

These stories illustrate that a successful transition through life's changes often requires respecting new boundaries while nurturing familiar intimacy. Efforts toward maintaining friendships involve a continuous dance between adjusting expectations and reaffirming the foundation of what makes those relationships worthwhile.

As we move forward, it's essential to reflect on questions like: How can we recalibrate closeness without harboring guilt over time apart? When is the right moment to reconnect, and how do we initiate that step comfortably? The strategies outlined so far offer insight into addressing such dilemmas. By maintaining regular communication, being flexible, leveraging technology, and appreciating the evolving nature of these bonds, friendships can thrive through the ebbs and flows of life. They remain strong, drama-free, and ultimately fulfilling over time.

When nurtured with care and intent, friendships transcend the challenges posed by life changes. It's about choosing each day to remember that relationships are living entities requiring time, attention, and adaptation, ensuring they flourish through transitions without losing their essence.

Friendship in Motion: Recalibrating Closeness

Navigating life changes can feel like a balancing act, especially when maintaining meaningful connections with friends. New jobs, relationships, or cities, even the joy and complexity of having kids, influence how we relate to those we hold dear. Yet, maintaining closeness sometimes requires recalibrating what that closeness looks like. Acknowledge that friendships naturally ebb and flow, much like the tides — sometimes you're in sync and close, and other times, life pulls you in different directions.

Recalibrating closeness starts with shedding guilt. Society often places unwritten rules about how friendships should be maintained, leading to feelings of guilt when the dynamic shifts. Instead of viewing distance as a sign of weakening ties, see it as an opportunity for growth in the relationship. Accepting the natural rhythm of friendship alleviates the pressure you and your friend might feel.

Understanding these shifts allows you to maintain equilibrium. It provides the freedom to ride the natural currents of life without the anchor of obligation dragging you down. Just as seasons change, so do our needs for support and connection. Recognizing that your best friend you once spoke with daily may now be someone you catch up with monthly doesn't diminish the bond; it merely adjusts to today's reality.

Timing is crucial for reconnecting after a period of absence. If you feel the drift between you and a friend, initiate a reunion when the moment feels right for both parties. Timing involves recognizing when your emotions and circumstances align for a meaningful interaction. Forcing a connection during personal chaos might create more distance instead of closing the gap. Respect your own and your friend's life pace, understanding that conditions for reconnection will vary.

Practical strategies for rekindling these bonds include the simple act of reaching out. A thoughtful message expressing your desire to reconnect can open the door without pressure. Instead of lengthy apologies for being away, focus on sharing mutual updates and plans. Maybe it's a coffee meetup when your schedules allow, or it's a long phone catch-up for those living further away. The key is to approach these interactions with genuine curiosity and enthusiasm for where your friend is presently in their life.

Adapting these strategies means viewing life changes not as interruptions but as opportunities to refresh and strengthen the friendship. Envision each reconnection as a renewal where you learn new aspects of your friend, enhancing the supportiveness of the bond. Appreciating the differences life brings to your companionship enriches the relationship, fostering growth at both individual and collective levels.

To illustrate, consider Jane and Tom, who have been friends since college. Jane moved to a new city after getting married. Distance and her new responsibilities meant less frequent communication with Tom. Initially, both felt the absence of their regular chats but understood that this change doesn't negate their friendship. The key lay in their acceptance of this drift. Eventually, Jane reached out with a casual invitation for Tom to visit her new city. The excitement of sharing her new life with him rekindled their bond, introducing new dimensions to their friendship.

The art of harmonizing distance and closeness hinges on open dialogue and empathy. Sharing with your friend how life changes affect your availability nurtures honesty. Encouraging them to express similar feelings fosters mutual understanding. This transparency goes a long way in aligning expectations, ensuring they happen on solid ground when reconnections occur.

These personal dynamics within a friendship are complex but manageable. They remind us that relationships aren't static. Instead, they evolve, echoing the broader theme of adapting to life changes. By integrating these approaches, you gain insight into managing friendships that withstand the test of time, regardless of the distances involved.

As we bridge into the following section, consider how these established friendships, maintained through evolving life circumstances, often face a unique challenge when romantic partners come into play. Sometimes, your partner might struggle to understand the nuances of your friendship. This situation calls for effective communication strategies and thoughtful boundary-setting. It's vital to forge a space where your friend and partner coexist harmoniously while retaining the integral parts of each relationship.

Next, we will explore ways to navigate these dynamics, focusing on the clarity and kindness necessary to maintain all connections healthily. We will delve into ensuring partners feel secure and friendships feel respected. Understanding how to handle these shifts will empower you to nurture relationships holistically; a skill invaluable to sustaining long-term connections in our ever-changing lives.

Managing Jealousy, Third Wheels, and Misunderstandings

In today's world, friendships face new challenges as we navigate romantic relationships alongside them. One recurring theme is the recalibration of closeness, significantly when life circumstances change. You might have experienced this when reconnecting with a friend after a prolonged distance, whether that distance was physical or emotional. These themes naturally lead us to a typical scenario where romantic partners sometimes see friendships as threats to their new or established relationship.

This perception often stems from the worry that friends might overshadow or take time away from what could be quality bonding moments in the romantic partnership. Such unaddressed concerns can snowball into misunderstandings or feelings of jealousy. Clear, honest communication is vital to manage these tensions without sacrificing the closeness you have established with your friends.

Imagine you recently started dating someone who feels uneasy about your long-standing Thursday night dinners with your closest friends. Open a dialogue instead of glossing over the issue or assuming they will get over it. Think about framing these dinners not as a threat but as an enhancement to your life, reminding your partner how these get-togethers recharge you and make you a better, more supportive partner. By reassuring your partner of their importance in your life, you disarm the potential for jealousy.

Now, how do you architect this negotiation? A strategy involves laying out the value of your friendship to your partner. Explain their role and history in your life in a way that resonates personally. Perhaps share anecdotes of how your friends were by your side through highs and lows. These stories illustrate the depth of your bonds, showing your partner why sustaining these connections is non-negotiable and beneficial for you as an individual.

Conduct this conversation when you and your partner are calm and open to discussion; preferably not when rushing out the door or late at night. Timing ensures the conversation is received as a meaningful exchange rather than an offhand comment. You reinforce the significance of these friendships while showing that your partner's sense of security is a priority.

Clear but kind boundaries stand as another layer of support. Set these boundaries early; it's much easier to maintain them than to establish them later when misunderstandings might have already sprouted. Articulate these boundaries in a way that's firm yet considerate. Perhaps you say, "I value my time with my friends and you, and there are spaces for both. Let's find a balance that respects what is important to each of us."

Decide what activities and aspects of your friendships are essential and non-negotiable. This clarity provides a roadmap for you and your partner, reducing room for conflict. Consider adapting your routines so they do not feel exclusionary to your romantic partner. If Thursday was traditionally dinner night, inviting your partner occasionally might dissolve some of their unease.

This discussion on managing friendships alongside romantic relationships naturally flows into integrating friendships into broader social circles. One effective method involves leveraging group dynamics. Here comes the concept of triads and platonic pods—structures that not only include but diversify social interactions.

Triads involve smaller groups where your romantic partner and close friends can engage in a relaxed setting, allowing for organic relationship building. It might mean inviting your partner and a friend to join you for a shared interest or hobby. Such setups provide non-threatening opportunities for interaction and shared experiences, highlighting commonalities rather than conflicts.

On the other hand, platonic pods revolve around slightly larger gatherings that keep interactions light and inclusive, emphasizing the autonomy and value of each relationship without overshadowing others. They offer the chance for your partner to see the positive dynamics firsthand; a firsthand view into why these friendships enrich your life.

These strategies help create an environment where romantic and platonic relationships thrive without stress. This balance ensures reduced drama and promotes an atmosphere of harmonious coexistence. People sometimes underestimate the power of a well-integrated social dynamic. It fosters understanding and empathy and drastically undercuts reasons for suspicion or jealousy before they take root.

All this preparation seamlessly sets the stage for that impending discussion on the broader theme of friendship integration moving from intimate navigations to more public or group-oriented dynamics. Such talks will explore incorporating these friendships into larger social frameworks, with an eye toward sustainability and enrichment for all parties involved.

The benefits are manifold. The inclusive structures of triads and platonic pods offer a unique avenue to keep interactions communal and light. This segues perfectly into exploring more collaborative and group-oriented friendship dynamics in the following section. Such practices go beyond past efforts, integrating friends and partners in meaningful ways that enhance social connections broadly and robustly. Prioritizing such interactions creates a foundation that carries through all aspects of your personal and social life, crafting a tapestry of interactions that build on shared histories and collective growth; a truly drama-free zone.

The Power of Group Dynamics and Conflict Repair

Successfully managing male-female friendships involves integrating them into your broader social circle. This helps maintain clarity and reduce misunderstandings in social contexts. Let's build on the idea of setting boundaries with romantic partners by examining how these friendships can thrive within a group setting.

The beauty of integrating a friendship into a bigger social circle is its ability to create a natural support system. It provides a communal environment where everyone benefits from shared interactions. Incorporating these friendships into triads or larger platonic pods can be particularly effective. These groupings ensure that interactions remain public, light, and inclusive, minimizing the risk of misinterpretation. Picture this: Jack and Emily have been friends for years. They maintain a healthy dynamic by attending group excursions, picnics, and casual get-togethers with their broader circle. Their friends recognize and support the platonic nature of their bond, leading to fewer misunderstandings.

These group interactions also prevent the friendship from becoming a source of tension in romantic relationships. For instance, a casual game night with multiple friends dilutes any perceived intensity that might arise from one-on-one meetings. When friendships are part of more fantastic social gatherings, those involved are less likely to feel trapped by societal expectations of male-female interactions. It is like surrounding oneself with a safety net of understanding and support.

Addressing potential conflicts within these friendships is crucial to their longevity. Every friendship encounters disagreements, but how those disagreements are managed defines the friendship's future. Directness and forgiveness are indispensable tools in resolving conflicts without jeopardizing the friendship. Direct communication ensures that issues are addressed head-on before they become insurmountable. Meanwhile, forgiveness allows the relationship to move forward without the baggage of past grievances.

Consider a scenario where Alex feels sidelined by Terry in a group activity. Alex might directly express feelings left out, allowing Terry to address the concern constructively. The conversation remains open and respectful, avoiding an unnecessary blow-up. By forgiving minor oversights, Alex and Terry reaffirm their commitment to maintaining their friendship. This openness strengthens their bond and prevents fractures from festering beneath the surface.

It's helpful to remember that problems will arise, but they don't have to spell the end. For example, Sarah and John's friendship faced turbulence when miscommunication led to a public argument. They addressed the issue privately, laying out their perspectives before reconciling. Their commitment to repairing their friendship highlighted resilience, showing that even severe disagreements can be surmounted. Recognizing the importance of managing these conflicts is essential for a drama-free relationship.

Understanding each other's perspectives and extending empathy during conflict resolution is essential. Acknowledging emotions involved in disagreements brings about resolutions grounded in respect and trust. It requires active listening and pausing judgment, focusing on the friendship's core values rather than the immediate conflict.

Integrating these friendships into larger social spheres and keeping interactions inclusive encourages transparency and trust. This clarity prevents misunderstandings, helping the friendship thrive without being weighed down by doubts. Maintaining public interactions also comes into play when fostering inclusivity, ensuring everyone feels like they belong without fearing judgment or disapproval. With this openness, friends maintain their boundaries while being part of a cohesive group.

Regarding supporting and uplifting one another, there's no doubt that friendships flourish in well-knit groups. Celebrating wins and offering solace during challenging times enriches the friendship, weaving it into the fabric of a larger dynamic. Think of it as having multiple people in your corner, ready to cheer you on or offer a listening ear. This supportive network fosters a positive environment, nourishing friendships and enabling them to thrive.

As we wrap up our discussion on integrating these friendships into broader social circles, it becomes apparent how these dynamics strengthen individual bonds and enrich the overall group environment. Friendships transcend individual encounters, adding layers of support and understanding. They thrive on shared experiences, creating a synergy that enhances personal connections.

But maintaining these friendships is not just about managing current dynamics and resolving conflicts; it's about understanding and anticipating the deeper aspects of connection that signify lasting partnerships. The next step in our journey involves delving into the complex interplay of emotional intimacy without expectations, mutual growth, and shared victories. These elements are what solidify the foundation of a lifelong bond. By weaving these aspects into the fabric of relationships, we pave the way for a deeper understanding of how friendships can adapt and thrive. Through mutual respect and shared experiences, these bonds evolve into lifelong partnerships, rich with understanding and empathy.

We will explore these dimensions as we move forward, recognizing how they contribute to relationships that endure and enrich our lives. Our next focus will be on the emotional layers that underscore long-term friendships, illumining how these connections symbolize the ultimate blend of support and mutual respect. With these insights, we will uncover friendships' potential to transform personal interactions and enhance the more expansive social tapestry they inhabit.

Signs of a Lifelong Bond

In the ebb and flow of friendships, incorporating these relationships into broader social circles often requires a juggling act, consulting calendars, compromising plans, and sometimes, negotiating through interpersonal conflicts. Integrating friends into more significant social scenarios builds a foundation of shared experiences, serving as an invaluable arena where bonds are tested and solidified. These experiences are critical in setting the stage for a deeper understanding of what makes a friendship genuinely enduring. Recognizing a lifelong bond often involves more than shared circles; it incorporates a blend of elements that resonate only in friendships mature enough to withstand time's test.

Emotional intimacy without expectation is one such cornerstone. Picture the kind of friend who asks, "How are you?" and genuinely wants an answer beyond the stock "fine." Within this realm, genuine emotional exchanges trump the need for reciprocity: a listener offering comfort without expecting the conversation to pivot back to their struggles immediately. Here's a scenario: Imagine a friend receiving the long-awaited promotion you two have talked about for years. A response layered with true joy reveals an emotional connection unburdened by jealousy or the compulsion to level the playing field with a comparable success story. This interpersonal dynamic demonstrates more than happiness for a friend's success; it underscores the freedom to express emotions authentically without the weight of unspoken expectations.

Next comes mutual growth and support during individual milestones, a signifier of durable friendships. Like the bonds formed in shared triumphs, connections are equally forged in life's inevitable setbacks. So, imagine a moment when one friend plans to embark on a daunting career change. The role of the other transforms into that of a confidant, helping to weigh the pros and cons and offering encouragement or a rational sounding board as needed. These shared navigations of life's complexities punctuate the bond, with each friend committed to standing by the other, not just in anticipation of potential success but in acknowledgement of the value intrinsic to the effort. As friends celebrate not just communal wins but individual triumphs and even missteps; they emerge on the other side, strengthened by the experience of mutual showing up.

Perhaps the most defining attribute of a lifelong friendship lies in its rarity and authenticity. Many of us pass through numerous social circles, with no shortage of acquaintances lighting up our contact lists or routinely appearing on our social media feeds. True friendship transcends these interactions, grounding itself as a relationship that values depth over breadth. Think about the conversations in which moments of distress can be shared without fear of judgment or the silent company kept on a lazy afternoon; evidence that connection need not be spoken to be felt. Such friendships display an unwavering authenticity; they acknowledge and celebrate individuality, accommodating evolution without the urge to eradicate differences.

These authentic connections are anchors during life's stormy trials and celebratory times. When calamity strikes; a job loss, health scares, or family turmoil, these rare friends form a familiar, unwavering refuge. They come bearing presence as a tonic rather than forced solutions or trite advice. Consider a scenario where tough decisions loom, and one friend insists, "No matter what, we'll figure it out together." In these moments, temporary solace paves the way for renewed strength, a testament to the friendship's enduring nature.

Life, ever replete with phases of highs and lows, calls upon friendships capable of mutual succession through changing dynamics. When one friend flourishes while the other falters, the balance of shared history fortifies the bond, providing a rich tapestry of experience from which to draw comfort and strength. Words of encouragement or quiet presence transform the experience of solitude into shared narrative threads, weaving a tapestry of understanding that advances friendship.

Importantly, as the clock hands spin, ticking away years that sometimes add distance or diversify interests, true friendships endure and flourish. Physical miles may widen, aspirations realign, and priorities shift. Yet, the importance of knowing there's someone who remembers you in your essence represents an intangible connection capable of transcending the most challenging intervals. Reunion brings familiarity akin to settling into one's favorite chair, a mix of comfort, history, and validation. These friendships remain vital as ever, standing unwavering amidst life's turning pages.

Friendships built on the signs of an enduring bond are life's gifts, sublime in their quiet strength yet never demanding ostentation. Emotional reciprocation, mutual support through growth challenges, and the rarity of authentic connections speak volumes when words may falter. The joy and affirmation of experiencing life with someone who champions your journey epitomize an enduring camaraderie that enriches us, standing as shields and scribes to life's narrative. Recognizing and nurturing these relationships remind us that true friendships, like the coves and caves that line our life's shoreline, hold their shapes against uncountable tides constants in an ever-shifting world.

Summary and Reflections

As we reflect on the dynamics of friendships amidst life's inevitable changes, we recognize that meaningful connections are built and preserved through intention and genuine effort. By maintaining consistent communication, embracing flexibility, and leveraging technology, friendships can adapt and thrive even when challenged by distance or evolving priorities. Now that we understand how vital it is to nurture these bonds actively, we can foster relationships that withstand time and grow richer with each transition. Strengthening our ability to recalibrate closeness without guilt, celebrating shared and individual milestones, and genuinely investing in one another's lives empowers us to keep our friendships strong and supportive, ensuring they remain drama-free and fulfilling over time. As we continue to navigate life's ebbs and flows, let us carry this insight, choosing each day to cherish and cultivate the friendships that enrich our journey.

EPILOGUE

As we reach the final pages of this journey into the depths of female communication and emotional intelligence, one thing becomes clear; understanding women is not about cracking a code or mastering a set of tactics. It's about connection, authenticity, and the willingness to listen, learn, and grow together.

Throughout this book, we've explored how women communicate, the importance of emotional attunement, and the key to fostering a meaningful and lasting relationship. We've unraveled the layers of verbal and nonverbal cues, dived into the power of empathy, and examined the deep-seated needs that drive women's desires for love and companionship. But ultimately, the most valuable lesson is this: relationships thrive on respect, effort, and emotional presence.

Understanding a woman isn't about being perfect; it's about being present. It's about showing up, not just physically but emotionally. It's about learning when to listen rather than respond, reassure rather than react, and be there without trying to fix everything. Women, like all people, want to feel valued, heard, and cherished. The more you prioritize those things, the deeper and more fulfilling your connection will be.

As you step away from these pages and into your relationships, remember that growth is continuous. Every conversation, every moment of understanding, and every shared silence is an opportunity to strengthen your bond. Keep curiosity alive, keep communication open, and keep showing up.

Ultimately, love isn't about knowing all the answers; it's about being willing to find them together. Nicci and I (Ben) agree to these principles.

The conversation never truly ends. It only deepens.

www.ingramcontent.com/pod-product-compliance
Lightning Source LLC
Chambersburg PA
CBHW061804120626
46550CB00005B/2132